The Cambridge Manuals of Science and
Literature

ENGLISH MONASTERIES

ST MARY'S ABBEY, YORK.
Crossing, north transept, and north aisle of nave.

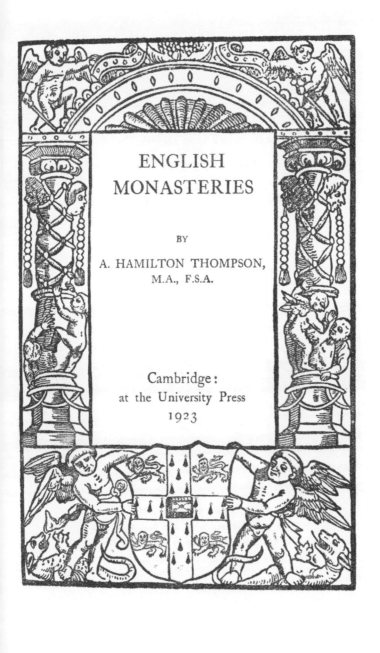

ENGLISH
MONASTERIES

BY

A. HAMILTON THOMPSON,
M.A., F.S.A.

Cambridge:
at the University Press
1923

CAMBRIDGE UNIVERSITY PRESS
Cambridge, New York, Melbourne, Madrid, Cape Town,
Singapore, São Paulo, Delhi, Tokyo, Mexico City

Cambridge University Press
The Edinburgh Building, Cambridge CB2 8RU, UK

Published in the United States of America by Cambridge University Press, New York

www.cambridge.org
Information on this title: www.cambridge.org/9781107620513

First published 1913
First Edition 1913
Second Edition 1923
First paperback edition 2011

A catalogue record for this publication is available from the British Library

ISBN 978-1-107-62051-3 Paperback

*With the exception of the coat of arms at
the foot, the design on the title page is a
reproduction of one used by the earliest known
Cambridge printer, John Siberch, 1521*

PREFACE

IN view of the growth of interest in medieval history and art, so conspicuous of late years, it is thought that this small volume may meet the needs of those who desire to know something about one of the most interesting sides of the life of the middle ages. There is no dearth of literature relating to monasteries, and the general facts of monastic history are accessible to the ordinary student in various handbooks. Monographs, however, which describe the plans of monasteries and the position and use of the principal buildings, exist for the most part in forms which are more difficult of access. Special attention has therefore been paid in the present case to the question of plan, and it is hoped that visitors to the remains of our English religious houses, who wish to gain some co-ordinate idea of their various parts, may find some help from this manual.

The writer desires to acknowledge gratefully the assistance of his wife, who is responsible for the plans and illustrations. The master of Emmanuel, the general editor of the series, has kindly read through the proofs and furnished valuable suggestions. The book has also had the great advantage of perusal and criticism by Mr W. H. St John Hope, Litt.D., D.C.L., to whose kindness and learning the writer is deeply indebted. Some idea of what students of English monastic life owe to Mr Hope may be gained from the bibliography at the end of this volume. Thanks are also due to the editors of the *Archaeological Journal* for permission to found the plan of Haughmond abbey (p. 114) on that by Mr H. Brakspear, F.S.A., in *Archaeol. Journal*, vol. LXVI.

A. H. T.

GRETTON, NORTHANTS.
12 *April*, 1913.

NOTE TO SECOND EDITION

The text in this edition has been revised, and the bibliography at the end of the book somewhat enlarged. Since the manual was first published, the death of Sir William St John Hope has deprived the author of the help of a kind friend upon whose advice and assistance he constantly relied.   A. H. T.

August, 1922.

CONTENTS

CHAPTER I

THE RELIGIOUS ORDERS

CHAPTER II

THE CONVENTUAL CHURCH

CHAPTER III

THE CLOISTER AND ITS BUILDINGS

CHAPTER IV

THE CISTERCIAN CLOISTER, ETC.

CHAPTER V

THE INFIRMARY AND THE OUTER COURT

CHAPTER VI

DISCIPLINE AND THE DAILY LIFE

LIST OF ILLUSTRATIONS

CHAPTER I

§ 1. A monastery is a community of men or women, devoted to the service of God and obeying a fixed rule. Monastic rules of life varied in strictness and in detail ; while each community supplemented the rule of its order by its own code of observances. The object, however, of these different rules and codes was one. The general term for the monastic life was 'religion' (*religio*): the 'religious' (*religiosus*) was bound by three vows, to poverty against the deceits of the world, to chastity against the lusts of the flesh, to obedience against the snares of the devil. His chief duty was to take part with his brethren in the recitation of the canonical hours, and in the celebration of daily masses. A portion of his day was set apart for meditation in the cloister ; but his surplus time was devoted to labour. The business affairs of a monastery brought some religious into touch with the practical side of life. Others found their vocation in manual labour in the fields or workshops ; while a certain number devoted themselves to literary work in the cloister.

§ 2.   The rule of St Benedict, on which western monachism was founded, distinguishes between four classes of religious.   Of these the two principal were cenobites, monks living in a community (*coenobium*) under rule, and the anchorites, who have departed (ἀναχωρεῖν) from the world to live a solitary life of prayer.   These were the sources of the two main streams of Christian monachism.   Naturally, the anchorite came first into existence.   The cenobite followed, by the combination of anchorites in monasteries.   The development of the *coenobium* was gradual.   About 305 A.D., St Anthony inaugurated the 'lauras' (λαῦραι) of northern Egypt, monasteries in which each anchorite lived in his separate cell and met for common services only on Saturday and Sunday.   A few years later St Pachomius founded his first *coenobium* at Tabennisi in southern Egypt. Here the social principle was more fully organised : common services in church were more frequent and labour was recognised as a factor in the monastic life ; but the monks still lived separately.   A further step was taken by St Basil, who about 360 founded a *coenobium* near Neocaesarea.   His rule introduced the idea of common life under one roof.   It became the basis of the monastic system of the eastern Church, and its principles had a lasting effect on the monastic life of western Europe.

§ 3.   The influence of the monachism of the east

naturally spread westward. No general rule of life was followed at first. Each collection of monks was governed by its own special observances, aiming generally at the ascetic ideal of separation from the world pursued by the early anchorites. Monachism, however, was a powerful agent in the Christianising of the west. Each monastery under its abbot or father became a training-ground for monk-bishops who ruled dioceses in new monastic centres of missionary effort. The beginnings of organised monachism in Ireland may be traced to the monastery of Lerins, on an island near Cannes, where St Patrick received his training. The success of Irish monasticism soon re-acted upon Gaul and Italy, when St Columban founded the monasteries of Luxeuil and Bobbio upon a rule derived from Irish practice. About the same time St Columba at Iona established the vogue of the Irish system in northern Britain.

§ 4. Meanwhile, a new development of the principle arose. St Benedict, a native of Norcia near Spoleto, retired about the beginning of the sixth century to a hermitage at Subiaco. Here he attracted a number of followers, and several monasteries arose in the neighbourhood under his direction. It was for the monastery of Monte Cassino, which he ruled for some thirty years, that he composed the rule which became the law of the monastic life of western Europe. The success and the general adoption of the rule of Monte Cassino in the west were due to the statesmanship with which its injunctions were adapted to climate and physical capacity. The Benedictine monk entered upon a life of work and prayer, which needed the habitual exercise of self-control; but his bodily health ran no risk of being ruined by pious excess. Isolated devotion was superseded by religious life in a common church and cloister. This was the end to which Pachomius and Basil had contributed; but the mystical temperament of the east fostered a contemplative and ascetic tendency which modified the conception of a common life of uniform duty. The early monasteries of Gaul, such as that of St Martin at Tours, followed the model of the *laura* rather than the *coenobium*; and the separate cell and the practice of self-imposed austerities seem to have been general in early Celtic monasteries. The voluntary hardships of St Cuthbert in his cell on the Farne islands, the prayers and visions of the Saxon Guthlac at Croyland, were western survivals of the ideals of St Anthony and St Simeon Stylites. St Benedict, on the contrary, while casting no reflexions on a life which he himself had at first adopted, recommended to the aspirant for salvation no heroic tasks of prayer and fasting. His aim was the growth in grace of a brotherhood, living under a common rule in obedience to an abbot to whom considerable discretion was given. The natural tendency of the solitary life was to produce an emulation in religious endeavour; and monasteries which were little more than collections of anchorites were liable to the decay consequent upon the rivalry of their inmates. St Benedict enjoined emulation in good works among his monks; but their emulation had its root in humility and obedience, and its outward sign was a mutual deference far removed from spiritual pride. There can be little wonder that a rule, difficult but possible to follow, and allowing for individual weakness, spread far outside the community for which it was made, and that the Benedictine order by the end of the seventh century supplanted all other forms of monasticism in western Europe.

§ 5. The rule of St Benedict was introduced into England by St Augustine, prior of the monastery on the Coelian hill in Rome. At this time the chief strength of Celtic monachism was naturally in the north, although it had penetrated southwards to such isolated outposts as Glastonbury. Gradually Roman customs gained ground in the strongholds of Celtic Christianity. The grant of the monastery of Ripon to Wilfrid was followed by the departure of the Scottish monks. Little is definitely known of English monastic life at this period, but it is clear that it began to approximate more closely to the Benedictine model. Thus the nuns of Hackness, an offshoot of

the monastery of Whitby, had a common dormitory;
while the monasteries of Monkwearmouth and Jarrow
differed in many respects from the local pattern, and
were certainly established upon a principle of common
life. In certain features a compromise seems to have
been arrived at, as in the survival of the custom,
which had probably been introduced by Irish mission-
aries, of grouping monks and nuns in one monastery
under the presidency of an abbess. The most famous
instance of this was the abbey of Whitby, but other
examples are known in various parts of England
remote from each other. For a few of these models
may have been found in Gaul, where the Benedictine
rule was not introduced until a period later than
the coming of Augustine. Another feature was the
establishment of bishops' sees in monasteries. In
European countries where the traditions of the Roman
occupation were more or less continuous, the cathedral
within the city was a distinct foundation from the
monasteries which, as at Paris or Rouen, rose at a
later date outside the walls. But the Celtic mission-
aries in England broke new ground in a country from
which the traces of Roman Christianity had almost
disappeared, and their sees were founded in monasteries. This custom was followed in the natural order
of things by Augustine at Canterbury. In the re-
organisation of dioceses after the Norman conquest
it was still continued. In eight of the seventeen

medieval dioceses of England the cathedral, and in two others one of the two cathedrals, was a monastic church.

§ 6. The Danish invasions brought extinction to the monastic life in the greater part of England. It was not until about a hundred years later that it was revived. Odo, archbishop of Canterbury 942–59, prepared the way for the movement. Its success was achieved under his successor, St Dunstan, with the co-operation of Edgar the peaceful. Ethelwold, bishop of Winchester, and Oswald, archbishop of York, were its most active promoters. Both were disciples of the reformed Benedictine rule which, early in the tenth century, had begun to spread from the abbey of Cluny. The abbey of Fleury or Saint-Benoît-sur-Loire, which, after the sack of Monte Cassino by the Lombards in 660, had become the resting-place of the body of St Benedict, was reformed under Cluniac influence. Oswald studied the Benedictine rule at Fleury. Made bishop of Worcester in 961, he was active in replacing the secular clergy of the churches of his diocese by monks. At Evesham, Pershore, Winchcombe, Worcester and elsewhere, Benedictine monks were introduced. In 971 Oswald aided Aelfwine, an East Anglian nobleman, to found the monastery of Ramsey in Huntingdonshire, and a few years later he and Ethelwold persuaded Abbo of Fleury to visit England

and help them in extending the religious life. Ethelwold was equally active at Winchester, and, under
a charter from king Edgar, restored destroyed
monasteries throughout the country, including Ely
and Peterborough. Dunstan, the reformer of Glastonbury, gave active sympathy to the movement, but
was more cautious in his attitude to the secular
clergy ; and it is noteworthy that the reform did not
at once extend to his cathedral church at Canterbury.

§ 7. This glorious period in the history of English
monasticism closed with the disasters of the early
part of the eleventh century. Canute and Edward
the Confessor favoured and enriched many religious
houses, and Edward, by his foundation of the abbey of
Westminster, takes a foremost place among benefactors of the religious life in England. But, during this
disturbed epoch, few new monasteries were founded,
and the tendency to slackness in observance of the
rule again appeared. The permanent triumph of
monasticism was achieved after the Norman conquest.
The Conqueror and his followers sought the salvation
of their souls by the foundation of abbeys and priories
on their new estates. The victory of Hastings was
marked by the foundation of the abbey of Battle,
the first of the long series of Norman monasteries in
England. In the work of organisation ecclesiastics
from the great abbeys of Normandy took, as was
natural, the chief part. Two successive archbishops

of Canterbury, Lanfranc, formerly a monk of Bec and abbot of St Stephen's at Caen, and Anselm, formerly abbot of Bec, were instrumental in giving the Benedictine order in England its pre-eminence under the early Norman kings.

§ 8. The Benedictine monasteries in England were colonised, or, where they were older than the conquest, received new blood from the monasteries of Normandy and France. We have seen that the rule of St Benedict was made for a special monastery: the order was a collection of independent houses which found the rule suitable to their needs. Thus each of the larger English Benedictine monasteries was a separate community, under the jurisdiction of the diocesan bishop, from whose visitations some powerful abbeys, such as St Albans, Evesham and Westminster, eventually obtained exemption. It was also subject to the visitation of two abbots, chosen annually by a general chapter of heads of English houses. The ruler of the monastery was the abbot: under him was his deputy, the prior, on whom a large part of the direct oversight of the house devolved. Where, as at Durham, the church of the monastery was also the cathedral of the diocese, the bishop was nominally abbot, but the actual ruler of the house was the prior; and to such houses the name of cathedral priory was given. The larger houses, however, frequently founded off-shoots on distant portions of their property, which were governed by priors appointed by the mother house, and were known as priories or cells. Although some of them became important houses, they were at first part and parcel of the mother house, and many continued to be so throughout the middle ages. Thus St Martin's at Dover was a priory of Christ Church, Canterbury, and Tynemouth in Northumberland was a priory of St Albans.

§ 9.   There were also certain priories founded in subordination to foreign houses. Thus Bec had a priory at St Neots in Huntingdonshire; the abbey of Mont-Ste-Cathérine at Rouen had one at Blyth in Nottinghamshire. Both these houses contained several monks: in the thirteenth century there were fourteen at Blyth, all probably foreigners, and many of them sent from the parent house for a change of air. But there were also a large number of monastic possessions known as priories, which were not strictly conventual, but were simply manors in the possession of alien monasteries, on which a prior or *custos*, sent from the mother abbey with another monk as his *socius*, resided for a portion of the year, practically as estate agent. Sometimes he was allowed, as at Ecclesfield in Yorkshire, a priory of Saint-Wandrille, to serve the cure of the parish church; but this was not common. Where these small 'alien priories' are known to have existed, we need not expect to find any trace of monastic arrangements in the parish church. Still less need we look for traces of a cloister. During the hundred years' war with France, the alien priories were repeatedly confiscated by the Crown, and before their final confiscation in 1414 many had been granted to English charterhouses, chantry colleges, and similar foundations. Conventual priories, such as Blyth and St Neots, were continued as independent monasteries under English priors.

§ 10. The popularity and wealth of the Benedictine order naturally led in many monasteries to relaxation of the rule. From time to time monks who felt the necessity of closer communion with God and a stricter life sought their need in the foundation of new houses under a more severe form of their rule. The first important move in this direction was made in the abbey of Cluny, from which, founded in 910, proceeded the monastic reform of the tenth century. St Berno, the first abbot, died in 927. One essential point distinguished Cluniac monasteries from Benedictine. Each Benedictine abbot was the president of his own republic. The Cluniac houses, on the other hand, were priories directly under the supervision of the abbot of Cluny, the autocrat of the order. They were exempt from episcopal visitation, and the abbot, holding his general chapters at Cluny, was responsible to the pope alone. In England their chief house was the priory of St Pancras at Lewes, founded in 1077 by William de Warenne for a prior and twelve monks: the prior of Lewes took second rank among Cluniac priors. Of some thirty-two English houses of the order several were cells of the larger priories, and at the general chapter would be represented by the priors of their parent monasteries. Owing to the dependence of the order upon Cluny, its English priories shared confiscation with the other alien foundations. They were allowed to continue, however, as 'denizen' houses with English priors, and the priory of St Saviour at Bermondsey was raised to the dignity of an abbey. Of ruins of Cluniac priories in England, the most complete are at Wenlock in Shropshire and Castle Acre in Norfolk. The plans of Lewes and Thetford priories have been recovered from foundations and fragments, and there are substantial remains at Bromholm in Norfolk.

§ 11.   The Carthusian order was founded by St Bruno at the Grande-Chartreuse near Grenoble in 1086.   Its members were vowed to fasting and the solitary life. Each had his separate cell, the monastery being composed of one or more courts, round which these dwellings were arranged. The brethren met in church for the night-office, mass, and vespers: the lesser hours were said, and meals, save on certain days, were taken by each monk separately. The order thus was a revolt against the common life, and a

return to the anchoritic ideal. In England only two
houses, Witham (*c.* 1179–81) and Hinton (*c.* 1227),
both in Somerset, were founded before the middle of
the fourteenth century. The remaining seven were
all founded after 1340. The royal foundation of
Shene priory in Surrey (1414) was the latest and
wealthiest of all. In England the word Chartreuse
(*Certosa* in Italian) took the form Charterhouse.
Considerable remains of charterhouses exist at
Beauvale in Nottinghamshire (founded 1343), in
London (founded 1371) and at Hinton; but the
most complete idea of a Carthusian priory may be
gained from the ruins of Mount Grace in Yorkshire
(founded 1396).

§ 12. One of the many off-shoots of the Benedictine
order was a congregation of monks and lay brothers
founded in 1114 in the diocese of Chartres. The name
of Thiron (*Tiro*) was given to the abbey from the
tirones or apprentices whom the founder united there,
to pursue their trades in the service of God. Closely
akin to this was the abbey of Savigny in the diocese of
Avranches, founded about 1105, which between that
date and 1147 planted some thirteen houses in England
and Wales. When the order of Savigny was merged
about 1147 in that of Cîteaux, its monasteries were
said to belong to the Tironensian order. This, however, was not because of any definite affiliation to
Thiron, but on account of similarity of observances

between the two congregations. English Tironensian houses, such as Humberston abbey in Lincolnshire, became identical with the ordinary Benedictine monasteries, although a nominal distinction was recognised. Important remains of a Tironensian house exist at Caldey, a priory of St Dogmaels, on an island near Tenby. Such Savigniac houses as Buildwas and Furness became famous as Cistercian monasteries. Neither of these congregations possessed the organising capacity which the founders of the Cistercian order brought to their work. The same may be said of the Grandimontine order, founded in 1046 at Grandmont in the diocese of Limoges, which during the twelfth century founded three small priories in England.

§ 13. The Cistercian order took its name from the abbey of Cîteaux in Burgundy, which was founded in 1098 by Robert, abbot of the Benedictine house of Molesme. His monks aimed at a literal observance of the rule of St Benedict on the most austere lines. Meat was banished from their meals: their buildings followed simple laws of construction and were free from ornament. The real founders of the order were Stephen Harding, an Englishman, who became abbot of Cîteaux in 1109, and his disciple St Bernard, who in 1115 became abbot of the first daughter house, Clairvaux. Largely owing to the energy of St Bernard, the order spread with extraordinary rapidity. When

Waverley abbey, its first English house, was founded in 1128, it possessed more than thirty houses. In 1152 an order forbade the foundation of new abbeys; there were then fifty houses in England and Wales out of 339. In spite of this prohibition, the number in the thirteenth century exceeded 600. In all, the houses of the order in England and Wales numbered 75, some of which possessed cells.

§ 14. Cîteaux, like Cluny, stood at the head of a federation of religious houses exempt from episcopal authority. These houses, however, were ruled by their own abbots, not by priors dependent on the abbot of Cîteaux; and thus the Cistercian abbeys were saved from the difficulties which befell the Cluniac in common with other alien houses. The Charter of Charity, drawn up in 1119, regulated the growth of the order and the relations between its monasteries. When the numbers of any house grew too large, it might, with the consent of the annual chapter at Cîteaux, send out at least twelve brethren, with a thirteenth as abbot, to found a new monastery. Thus Waverley was colonised from the abbey of L'Aumône in Normandy. Fountains, founded in 1132 and augmented from Clairvaux in 1134 or 1135, sent out colonies to Newminster in Northumberland (1138), Louth Park in Lincolnshire (1139), Woburn in Bedfordshire (1145) and Lysa in Norway (1146). The right of visitation of Cistercian houses belonged to

the abbots of their parent monasteries: the abbot
of Cîteaux was visitor of Clairvaux, the abbot of
Clairvaux visitor of Fountains, and so on; while
Cîteaux itself was visited by the abbots of Clairvaux
and its three other eldest daughters. Monasteries
thus founded were to be in places remote from the
conversation of men. Such names as Vaudey (*Vallis
Dei*) and Valle Crucis mark the favourite site of
such abbeys in secluded valleys: it was seldom that
the rule was transgressed, as in the case of St Mary
Graces near the tower of London. The churches
were dedicated in honour of our Lady: stone bell-
towers were forbidden as well as wooden towers of
excessive height, the windows were filled with plain
glass, all paintings were prohibited save painted
wooden crucifixes, and vestments and other ornaments were of the plainest kind compatible with
dignity. All workshops, stables, etc. were within
the abbey precincts, and precautions were taken
against the growth of any colony of lay-folk near
the monastery by the order that any house built
outside the precinct wall was to be pulled down.
A similar precaution regulated the establishment of
the abbey farms or granges at a specified minimum
distance from each other. Temporary guests were
admitted under special conditions; but, after the
dedication of the church and its octave were over, the
presence of women within the precinct was forbidden.

§ 15.   One point in the Cistercian rule, which arose from this self-contained ideal and had an important influence upon the planning of Cistercian buildings, was the division of the brethren of each abbey into monks (*monachi*) and lay brothers (*conversi*)[1]. The Cistercian monk was a clerk who could read and write. Like a Benedictine monk, he was not necessarily a priest, although it became very general for monks to proceed to priest's orders. His duties lay in the church and cloister, and, unless he held an office such as that of cellarer or kitchener, he was not immediately concerned with the business affairs of his convent. These, which in Benedictine houses were largely transacted by tenants or hired labourers and servants, were performed in Cistercian houses by the *conversi*. A *conversus* was a layman who had turned from the service of the world to that of God. He entered the convent as a novice and in due course made his profession. He was precluded from learning to read or write and from taking holy orders. He was taught a few prayers and psalms by heart, but his business was manual labour in the convent workshops, or in its fields and granges. On

---

Conversi were found in houses of other orders, e.g. the Augustinian, but their position in such cases was less definite than in the Cistercian order. Male *conversi* were attached to houses of Cistercian nuns: examples of this are known in Lincolnshire and Yorkshire.

ordinary work-days he had to attend part of the night-office and, if he was not stationed in a grange, had to come to compline. He observed the other hours by the recitation of special prayers at his work. His life was regulated by statutes which in respect of abstinence, silence and other similar essentials resembled those of the monks. The *conversi* had their own separate common rooms in the cloister buildings, their own quire in the church and their own infirmary. They rose at an hour which was specially calculated to allow them enough sleep before their day's work: their chapter was held by the abbot only on Sundays and certain feast-days. Thus the convent was provided with all the workmen whom it needed. Some *conversi* were deputed to live upon the convent granges, each of which had a *conversus* as prior. The white frocks and cowls of the monks gave the Cistercians their distinctive name of white monks as opposed to the Benedictines or black monks: the dress of the *conversus* was a cloak (*cappa*), tunic, stockings (*caligae*), boots (*pedules*) and a hood (*capucium*) covering only the shoulders and breast[1].

---

[1] In 1301 the Benedictine monks of Gloucester were allowed a frock and cowl out of the wardrobe at least once a year, day-shoes once in 18 months, boots once in five years, pairs of woollen shirts (*langelli*) once every four years. They could change when necessary a thick and thin tunic, their pilch or fur cloak (*pellicea*), ordinary boots, under-shirt (*stamen*) and drawers (*femoralia*).

§ 16.   The monastic movement was not in the
first instance a clerical movement, nor can the earliest
founders have contemplated that their convents would
include more than a few priests for the ministration
of the Sacraments.   But the ideal of the regular life
as pursued in the monasteries attracted clergy as well
as laymen.   As early as 391, St Augustine established
communities of regular clergy in Africa.   In the later
years of the eighth century, Chrodegand, bishop of
Metz, introduced a rule of life, founded upon that of
St Benedict, among the clergy of his cathedral, which
was copied by other similar congregations of clergy.
From the official list on which their names were in-
scribed (*canon*, κάνων) the members of such bodies
became known as canons, and the bodies themselves,
meeting in chapter-houses, where a chapter (*capitulum*)
of the rule was read daily, took the name of chapters
(*capitula*).   The main object of the movement was
the daily recitation of the canonical hours : the
canons had their meals in common, and in some cases
had a common dorter or dormitory.   The tendency
during the ninth and tenth centuries seems to have
been for canons to establish their separate households
in the neighbourhood of the church which they served.
A marked distinction arose between the monks of
cathedral priories such as Canterbury and the secular
canons who served such churches as the cathedral of
York.   In the secular chapters the recitation of the

hours was maintained and certain common funds
were administered; but each canon had his own
separate estate, a church or manor known as a
prebend (*prebenda*), and the richer prebends became
the perquisites of clerks in constant attendance upon
the king or upon some bishop or nobleman. The
number of resident canons was very small, and the
duties of absentees were taken by their vicars (*vicarii*)
or deputies. Colleges of chantry-priests, usually of
late foundation, were organised as similar associations
of secular clergy, who were bound, however, from the
nature of their duties to continual residence. The
colleges of Oxford and Cambridge had a similar basis.
They were associations of clergy for teaching and
study, with a common hall and church, and are therefore derived from a source distinct from the monastic
movement.

§ 17. Bodies of canons regular, however, came
into existence, distinct from the chapters of canons
secular, living in monasteries, reciting the canonical
hours, and leading the common life of monks. Their
rule was modelled on an adaptation of a letter from
St Augustine of Hippo to a congregation of religious
women. It was shorter and couched in more general
terms than the rule of St Benedict; but its aim
was similar. Its followers became known as Augustinian or Austin canons. From their hooded black
cloaks with white surplices and black cassocks

beneath, they were often called black canons. The order did not appear in England until about 1106, when the priory of St Botolph at Colchester was founded by a Benedictine monk named Ernulf; nor did the papacy definitely recognise the order until 1139, when its houses were already numerous. The number of English Augustinian houses at its highest point reached 218, and of these 138 were founded before 1175. At the suppression of the monasteries there were about 170 Augustinian houses, while of Benedictine houses there were from 130 to 140. Augustinian houses varied greatly in size and wealth, and at no time did their wealthier abbeys approach the immense revenues of the greater Benedictine houses ; while their average income was very moderate. Each house was governed by a 'prelate,' generally known as the prior, but in some 24 cases as the abbot. Most of their abbeys were in the midland districts: in Yorkshire, Nottinghamshire and Norfolk, where their houses were numerous, the title of prior was universal. In 1133 one of their convents, Carlisle, was raised to the dignity of a cathedral priory. Their growth was analogous to that of the Benedictines : each house with its cells was an independent community : their visitor was the diocesan bishop, and very few of their houses became permanently exempt from visitation. The order also held its general chapters, at which two visitors were appointed yearly for each of the provinces into which its houses were divided.

§ 18. The order of Premonstratensians, known from their white habit as white canons, was founded by St Norbert at Prémontré, to the west of Laon, about 1120. The canons followed the Augustinian rule in the main, but their constitution shewed a tendency to follow Cistercian models. The order was centralised under the abbot of Prémontré, where the general chapters were held, and was extended by the Cistercian process of colonisation, each house sending out its body of canons as the nucleus of a new abbey. Lisques, a daughter of Prémontré, colonised Newhouse abbey in north Lincolnshire in 1143. In 1147 Newhouse founded a daughter house at Alnwick, and between that time and 1212 founded ten other abbeys. Of these Welbeck (1153) was responsible for seven more between 1175 and 1218. In all there were thirty-one abbeys of the order in England, not counting two cells. Cistercian influence can be seen in the constitution of each new house as an abbey, in the choice of secluded sites for the houses of the order, and in the principal dedication of most of its churches to our Lady. Like other centralised orders, the Premonstratensians were exempt from the jurisdiction of the diocesan bishop; but the allegiance of the English canons to Prémontré gradually slackened, and the administration of their order in England was delegated in course of time to a commissary. In 1512 Julius II exempted the English houses from obedience to Prémontré and placed them under the control of the abbot of Welbeck.

§ 19. The order of Prémontré originally made some provision for houses of nuns side by side with those of canons. The experiment languished, and although a body of nuns or canonesses followed the Premonstratensian rule, they had few houses. Only two are known in England, and neither of these was connected with any house of canons. But in the second quarter of the twelfth century Gilbert, rector of Sempringham in Lincolnshire, with the advice of the abbot of Rievaulx, founded a house of seven nuns following the Cistercian rule. The Cistercian order refused to take charge of the community, and Gilbert, possibly following the example of Prémontré, provided for its spiritual needs by associating with the nuns a body of canons under the rule of St Augustine. Gilbertine houses were thus at first regarded as nunneries in which the Sacraments were administered by an auxiliary community of at least seven canons. Minutely composed statutes provided for the seclusion of the two bodies from each other in two adjacent cloisters. In such double houses the maximum number of nuns ordained by statute was generally double that of canons: thus at Watton in Yorkshire, the largest house of the order, nominal provision was made for 140 nuns and 70 canons. The order, which was exempt from episcopal control, was placed under a general, known as the master of Sempringham. Sempringham was the mother house of a number of priories : new houses were founded on the Cistercian plan of the migration of twelve canons and a prior from one of the existing houses. *Conversi* and *conversae* formed a part of each establishment. The total number of Gilbertine houses was some 27, of which eleven were in Lincolnshire : with the exception of one house in Wiltshire, and one on the border of Wiltshire and Gloucestershire, the monasteries of the order were all within the four eastern dioceses of Lincoln, York, Ely and Norwich. The order never spread beyond England.

§ 20. Houses of Benedictine nuns were numerous in England. The most important of these lay within the dioceses of Salisbury and Winchester. In the midlands, the east and north, where they were numerous, they were with a few exceptions small foundations of which scanty traces are left. A few priories of nuns, chiefly in the dioceses of York and Lincoln, followed the Cistercian rule. In the sixteenth century the wealthiest of the Cistercian nunneries, which as a rule were small and poor, was at Tarrant in Dorset; and it has been supposed till lately that it was for three nuns who originally settled here that the famous *Ancren Riwle* was composed. Cistercian nunneries were not subject to Cîteaux, but were visited by their diocesan bishop. Houses of nuns or canonesses following the rule of St Augustine were few; but of their two abbeys, Burnham and Lacock, there are substantial remains. The richest nunnery at the suppression was Sion abbey in Middlesex, founded by Henry V in 1414 for Bridgetine nuns, whose rule was modelled on that of St Augustine. The Bridgetine order, as well as that of Fontevrault, to which Nuneaton priory in Warwickshire originally belonged, attempted to provide regular chaplains for its members by uniting a convent of men to one of women. In connexion with some of the older Benedictine nunneries there were from an early date secular chaplains who had their own prebends in the monastic estates and their stalls in quire. In process of time such prebendal stalls in the churches of Romsey, Shaftesbury, Wilton, Wherwell and St Mary's, Winchester, became perquisites of clerks in the royal service, whose duties in the nunneries were performed by vicars.

§ 21. After the beginning of the fourteenth century the foundation of monasteries practically ceased, although the Carthusian order at a later date enjoyed some popularity, which was enhanced by royal patronage. Religious houses no longer afforded the only career possible to those who were unfitted for the limited professions open to the medieval layman. With the growth of a well-to-do middle class came the tendency to devote benefactions which at an earlier date would have been given to monasteries to parish churches. From the reign of Edward II onwards chantries and colleges of chantry-priests in parish churches were founded in great numbers. In one respect, however, the regular life kept in touch with national progress. The orders of friars found their way to England in the thirteenth century. In 1221 Dominicans (Friars preachers or black friars) settled at Oxford: about 1224 houses of Franciscans (Friars minor or grey friars) were established at Canterbury and London: Hulne priory in Northumberland and Aylesford priory in Kent were founded for Carmelites (white friars) about 1240: Clare priory in Suffolk was founded for the order known later as Austin friars in 1248. Some lesser orders of canons, such as the Trinitarian, whose most famous house was at Knaresborough, are sometimes classed with friars. Although the general plan of a friary was similar to that of a monastery, the lives of monks and friars were totally different. The friar was a wanderer who lived on alms: his circuit was bounded by a special province, and he was not confined to the limits of a single house. The favourite places for friaries were thus the larger towns. No less than seven houses of friars were founded in Cambridge: there were six each in London and Oxford: Bristol, Lincoln, Lynn, Newcastle,

Northampton, Norwich, Stamford, Winchester and
York contained houses of all the four chief orders. An
order of nuns, known as the Poor Clares from their
foundress St Clare, was an off-shoot of the Franciscan
order, and had five houses in England. The influence
gained by these new bodies served to turn popular
attention from the older orders. Not merely were
the friars the revivalist preachers of the age, in
antagonism to the conservative spirit of the monks
and secular clergy[1]; but the great learning of many of
their leading members earned them distinction and
no little weight in the universities of Europe. The
moral dangers of their life, their independence of
episcopal control and their unchecked influence
among the common people brought about an early
decline from the ideals of their founders; but their
achievements during the first century of their existence are one of the most remarkable episodes in
religious history.

§ 22. Although monks and canons were bound to
individual poverty and all who attempted to accumu-
late a private store of money were liable to punishment,

[1] In 1230 the monks of St James', Bristol, a cell of Tewkesbury,
petitioned the bishop of Worcester against the consecration of the
Dominican church in St James' parish. Various documents in the
York episcopal registers between 1279 and 1296 deal with the rivalry
between the *custodes* of the alien priory of Scarborough and the local
Dominicans. In both cases the root of ill-feeling was the diversion
by the friars of the oblations due to the parish altar.

the greater monasteries were large landowning corporations. Their early benefactors bestowed gifts of manors and churches upon them for which they were bound in return to the sole service of praying for the souls of the donors. Such alienations were regulated by the statute of mortmain (1279). Benefactions continued under the procedure established by this act, and the monasteries thus became owners of a very large number of parish churches. The custom of appropriation and its effects on the fabrics of parish churches has been stated in another volume of this series[1]. The constant plea for appropriation was founded on the insufficiency of the funds of a monastery to fulfil its duty of hospitality to wayfarers and of relief to the poor. In churches of which monks were proprietors, the vicar was a resident secular priest. Monks were not allowed, save in very exceptional cases, to serve the cures of parishes, which would have interfered with their duties in quire and cloister. Wherever we find it stated in print that an incumbent of a parish church or chantry was a monk, we should hesitate to believe it without consulting the original record of his institution. Canons, on the other hand, whose orders began in the association of secular priests under a rule, were given more licence in this respect. Premonstratensian canons were

[1] *Historical Growth of the English Parish Church*, 1911, pp. 11–15.

generally allowed to serve the parish churches belonging to their houses; and bishops granted similar licences, though not without demur, to Austin canons. It is sometimes stated that the object of the Augustinian order was to supply parochial clergy to churches on their estates. If this was so, the custom was severely checked in the thirteenth century; and, when in the later middle ages the number of appropriated churches served by Austin canons considerably increased, the quire services in their monastic churches suffered to an extent which was never contemplated by their founders.

§ 23. The position of monasteries as landowners naturally led to some slackening of the rule. Abbots and priors of the larger houses took their place among the spiritual barons of the realm. From the fourteenth century to the suppression twenty-four Benedictine and three Augustinian abbots, with the prior of Coventry and the English prior of the knights hospitallers, had a prescriptive right to seats in parliament. These are sometimes confounded with 'mitred' abbots: the right, however, of an abbot or prior to wear episcopal insignia depended, not upon a parliamentary summons, but upon a privilege granted by the pope. In addition to the extra-monastic duties thus incumbent upon certain heads of houses, the care of large estates took many of the brethren away from constant attendance in their house. When bishop

Alnwick of Lincoln visited Peterborough abbey in 1437, he found that out of 44 monks there were seldom on ordinary days more than ten or twelve at any service in church. The obedientiaries or officers who looked after the chief departments of the convent came to church only on great festivals: some monks lived upon the abbey granges: every week at least seven were on furlough for blood-letting: two were at their studies at Oxford: several were old and infirm and could not attend service regularly. The somewhat trite remark of the cellarer at Leicester in 1440 that 'abundance of money is the cause of many evils' is justified over and over again in the records of episcopal visitations.   In spite, however, of their wealth, even the richest houses, as a rule, were beset by money difficulties.   Their expenses were great: hospitality and the daily alms were a serious drain on income: pensions and corrodies or shares in the common revenue were too liberally granted to outsiders: there was much necessary outlay on property: young monks had sometimes to be maintained in hostels belonging to monasteries at the universities : an ambitious abbot might run his house into extravagant expense on buildings: episcopal visitations meant a large fee to the bishop and expense upon his entertainment. The improvidence of officers, joined with the damage caused to property by pestilence and storm, constantly reduced monasteries to a state of bankruptcy.   The heavy debts of monasteries, their insufficient assets, the irregularity with which accounts were rendered, and the consequent decay of discipline are abundantly illustrated in the registers of fourteenth and fifteenth-century bishops and in the patent rolls of the reigns of Henry V and Henry VI.

§ 24. *'Decem sunt abusiones claustralium,'* runs an inscription upon the quire-stalls of St Agatha's abbey, now in Richmond church, 'The abuses of those in cloister are ten: costly living, choice food, noise in cloister, strife in chapter, disorder in quire, a neglectful disciple, a disobedient youth, a lazy old man, a headstrong monk, a worldly religious.' The actual evidence of documents, when compared with the counsels of perfection in the rules of orders and the custom-books of monasteries, supplies a commentary on this text which applies to every century from the thirteenth to the sixteenth. It must also be owned that grave moral offences were not uncommon. Where slackness of rule was prevalent, temptations of this kind must have abounded, and convents which had the misfortune to possess an unworthy or lazy head were liable to succumb to them. Such weaknesses, however, are just those on which satirists lay excessive emphasis and to which scandal lends a too ready ear. The evidence of episcopal visitations, while it discloses much that is repellent to our ideal of the religious life, seldom proves that moral corruption

was general in any given monastery, or that individual
backslidings went without punishment. Cases of
immorality, though not few, are generally treated
with an individual prominence which would be impossible, if a whole monastery were implicated in
them. This fact must be laid against the credence
which is still sometimes given to the so-called *com-
perta* of Henry VIII's commissioners, the trustworthi-
ness of which is now rightly discredited. Bishops
like Alnwick would spend months of hard work in
visitations and several days, if necessary, on the im-
partial examination of the evidence for a single crime,
while such commissioners as Dr Layton rushed at full
speed through the monasteries committed to their
inquiry, with prejudices already formed and with the
most casual examination of witnesses, enforcing
resignations of abbots and extorting confessions and
bribes from frightened monks and nuns, with the
closely allied objects of bringing the revenues of
the houses to the royal exchequer and of earning
grants of prebends and deaneries for themselves.

§ 25.   There can be no doubt, however, that during
the fourteenth and fifteenth centuries the life of
monks and canons regular became generally more lax
and easy, while the numbers of those who embraced
the monastic life decreased.   In the twelfth century
the monasteries had been full to overflowing : each
newly-founded house was a sign that the parent

monastery had no more room.   In the middle of the
thirteenth century the numbers were still large but
not unwieldy.   Such numbers as we have indicate
that the monasteries were kept up to the complement
of inmates required by their statutes, but that there
was no general increase.   In Cistercian abbeys the
number of *conversi* swelled the total of inmates: at
Louth Park during the same period there were 66
monks, while the *conversi* numbered 150[1].   Such
numbers, however, decreased greatly within the next
hundred years.   In 1349, the year of the great
pestilence, there were 42 monks at Meaux, but only
seven *conversi*: 32 monks and all the *conversi* died.
The pestilence worked similar havoc in other houses.
In the small nunnery of Wothorpe, near Stamford,
only one nun was left: Greenfield priory in Lincolnshire remained without a head for three months.
There can be little doubt that the religious houses as
a whole never recovered from the pestilence: there
were not enough recruits from outside to compensate
for the sudden decrease in numbers.   Alnwick's visitations in the middle of the fifteenth century shew that
the monasteries of his diocese were far from full.

---

[1] At Waverley, late in the twelfth century, there were 70 monks,
120 *conversi*.   That the monks sometimes found the *conversi* difficult
to manage is shewn by the action of abbot Richard (1220–35) at
Meaux, who removed them from the granges and confined them to
menial and craftsmen's work.

Later visitations in the diocese of Norwich strengthen
the conclusion that even in important houses like the
cathedral priory of Norwich a number of from 40 to
50 monks was exceptionally large. In 1492 there were
only 17 canons in the wealthy priory of Walsingham.
In the largest Premonstratensian houses, during the
last quarter of the fifteenth century the numbers
seldom exceeded 25. The distinction between the
various orders was no longer clearly marked. After
1349 *conversi* ceased to form a part of most Cistercian
monasteries. Within the next fifty years they disappeared altogether, and the monks, like the Benedictines, administered their estates by hired labour.
At the suppression of the monasteries the number of
monks at Furness, where the accommodation was
unusually large, was only 30. In Bury St Edmunds,
one of the largest Benedictine abbeys, there were
about 60.

§ 26. The decline in numbers after 1349 would
inevitably tend to the extinction of small and poor
houses. A few nunneries, such as Wothorpe, were
amalgamated with larger foundations. Various causes
also led to the suppression of small monasteries. An
example had been set as early as 1312 by the exter-
mination of the military order of knights Templars,
whose rule was founded upon the Cistercian *Carta
Caritatis*. Their lands in great part went to enrich
the order of knights of St John of Jerusalem, whose

property at the general suppression was very large. During the French wars, as we have seen, the smaller possessions of foreign abbeys were gradually appropriated to other religious foundations. Alien priories also formed a large portion of the possessions of Eton and King's college, Cambridge. For the purposes of later colleges at Oxford and Cambridge, this example was followed in the suppression of small English houses : Jesus college at Cambridge in 1497 entered upon the buildings and possessions of the nunnery of St Radegund. Wolsey founded Christ Church at Oxford in place of the priory of St Frideswide, and obtained the suppression of several small monasteries for the endowment of his colleges at Oxford and Ipswich. To Wolsey indeed the beginning of the general suppression may be fairly attributed. His measures, however, had reform for their end. Later acts of suppression were prompted by far different causes. Yet not even the financial advantages of the step could lead to the destruction of the monasteries at one blow. The act of 1536 put in the king's hands only those houses whose revenues were under £200 a year, and of these thirty-two, against which even the commissioners could find no evidence, were refounded. Such an act naturally produced serious economic changes: the ringleaders of the subsequent northern rebellion complained of the damage incurred by the poor from the loss of convent alms. The Pilgrimage of Grace brought disaster to the abbeys which had lent it support. Other houses made terms with the king by surrendering their possessions: the rest fell in consequence of the act of 1539, which extended the provisions of 1536 to all the surviving foundations. It may be granted that the dissolution of the monasteries was inevitable. But for their arbitrary seizure by the state there was only the shadow of a legitimate reason, and the motives of the suppression are exposed by the traffic in their property which followed. Pensions were granted to monks and canons from the exchequer; but the bulk of monastic property went to enrich private owners for the temporary relief of the extravagance of the Crown.

§ 27. Many monasteries were entirely ruined after the suppression, and of about a third of the number no vestige is left. Of rather less than a third there are substantial remains. In many cases, these are confined to the church, which, if it served the needs of a parish, was granted to the parishioners and partially used by them, the monastic quire being generally allowed to go into decay. More rarely, as at Christchurch priory, the whole church was retained. Secular chapters were founded in the cathedral priories, and six abbey and priory churches, including Westminster, were raised to the rank of cathedrals. Thus, allowing for the inevitable change of use to which the monastic buildings were put, at Canterbury, Chester, Durham, Ely, Gloucester, Norwich, Peterborough, Rochester, Westminster, Winchester and Worcester, the arrangements of a Benedictine monastery can be studied more or less satisfactorily, and at Bristol, Carlisle and Christ Church, Oxford, those of a house of Austin canons may be fairly well seen. Of ruined houses by far the most complete series of remains are those of the Cistercian abbeys, which, generally in remote situations, have been allowed to go to decay with little removal of material. Benedictine, Cluniac and Augustinian houses have suffered more: the remains of Benedictine houses like Reading or St Mary's, York, are not complete ; while of Cluniac houses Wenlock, and of Augustinian, Haughmond and Lilleshall are some of the few exceptions to the general rule of destruction. Only three Cistercian churches remain partly in use as parish churches, viz. Dore, Holme Cultram and Margam: they were converted to this use at periods later than the suppression. On the other hand, the remains of nearly half the monasteries enable us to reconstruct the life which was led in them with great completeness. Pre-eminent among these is the magnificent ruin of Fountains. Kirkstall and Tintern are hardly less complete. Beaulieu, Buildwas, Cleeve, Croxden, Ford, Furness, Jervaulx, Neath, Netley, Valle Crucis and Rievaulx have singularly perfect remains of large

portions of the cloister buildings, and to these may
be added several other instances where churches
or other buildings remain or may be traced by
foundations. Traces of most of the Premonstratensian houses are left. The most perfect is the
splendid abbey of St Agatha at Easby near Richmond.
Part of one Premonstratensian church, that of Blanch-
land in Northumberland, has been converted into
a parish church. Of Carthusian plans, as already
said, much is known, and for completeness Mount
Grace priory is not far behind Fountains. One
Gilbertine plan, that of Watton in Yorkshire, has
been recovered by excavation. Of houses of nuns the
remains are somewhat scanty, but of Benedictine
foundations St Radegund's priory at Cambridge, and
of Augustinian houses Lacock abbey in Wiltshire
deserve special mention ; while the great Benedictine
church of Romsey abbey remains entire. Fragments
of friaries are left in many of our large towns : of
their general arrangements much can be seen at the
Dominican friary in Bristol and in the ruins of the
Austin friary at Clare and the Carmelite friary at
Hulne. The church of the Austin friars in London
is still a place of worship: the quire of the Dominican
friary at Brecon is the chapel of Christ college. Fragments of churches may be seen at Lynn (black friars)
and Richmond (grey friars), while the church of the
Dominicans at Norwich and that of the Franciscans

at Chichester have been converted to secular uses. At Cambridge the colleges of Emmanuel and Sidney Sussex were founded on the sites of Dominican and Franciscan friaries. The Dominican buildings at Emmanuel were cleverly adapted to the plan of the new college, the hall of which, in spite of transformation, is substantially the church of the friary.

CHAPTER II

THE CONVENTUAL CHURCH

§ 28. The precinct of a religious house was separated from the outer world by an enclosing wall or dyke, on the line of which a gatehouse gave admission to the outer court (*curia*). Here were placed various offices and storehouses, and such buildings as the almonry and guest-house, in which the monastery came into necessary contact with secular affairs. The church and cloister, devoted to the religious life, occupied approximately the middle of the precinct, the cloister and its surrounding buildings being generally placed on the south side of the nave of the church. At the east end of the church was the graveyard ; while outside the cloister was a collection of buildings, sometimes arranged round a court or smaller cloister, of which the chief

was the infirmary. In dealing with these divisions,
the church and cloister, the centre of the daily life of

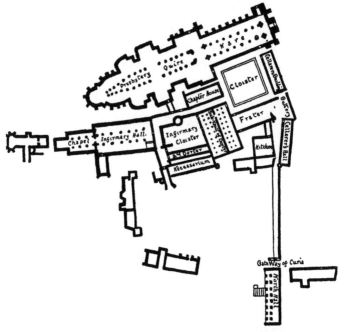

Fig. 1.   Plan of the cathedral priory, Canterbury
(after Professor Willis).

the monastery, must be taken first.   It is necessary to
remember that while the relative position of *curia*,

cloister and infirmary buildings was almost always
the same, their actual position varied according to
the site of the monastery. The natural place for the
curia was on the west side of the church and cloister,
and in Cistercian monasteries, where the site was un-
encumbered by other buildings, it is usually found in
this position. On the other hand, as at Durham and
Worcester, where the site was longer from north
to south than from east to west, the *curia* was on
the south side of the cloister. Again, where a
monastery was founded on the north side of a town,
as at Canterbury, Chester and Gloucester, it was
convenient that the cloister should be on the
north side of the church, where seclusion and
quiet were possible. Occasionally, as at Tintern,
where a river ran north of the abbey, the cloister
was placed on that side for purposes of drainage;
while in a few instances a river on the west side
of the cloister was the cause of important variations
in the plan of the buildings. In one exceptional
case, at Rochester, the confined nature of the site
led to the building of the cloister on the south side
of the eastern arm of the church.

§ 29. The position of the chief buildings round
the cloister was arranged upon a convenient principle,
which commended itself to monks and canons alike.
The chapter-house was always in the eastern range of
buildings: the dormitory or dorter was nearly always

on the first floor of the same range: the refectory or
frater was always in the range opposite the church[1].
This was the usual Benedictine plan, and its dis-
positions, allowing for some variation, were followed
by most of the religious orders. But the Cistercian
order, while maintaining the relative position of
the cloister buildings, developed a special type of
church and plan of cloister, which were in no small
degree the result of its peculiar constitution. Its
claustral arrangements were peculiar to itself, but its
church-plan had some effect upon the churches of
other orders, particularly upon those of Premonstratensian canons. In considering the monastic church,
it will be useful in the first place to take the main
features of the Benedictine plan, and in the sequel,
after noting the peculiarities of Cistercian churches,
to observe the effect of both plans on the churches of
other orders. In all monastic churches, however, the
plan was governed by three common necessities.
(1) A quire had to be provided for the recitation of
the canonical hours by the convent. (2) A sufficient

---

[1] The order in which the parts of a monastery were built
followed the immediate needs of the convent. Thus at Evesham
the eastern part of the church and the eastern range of the cloister
were built first: the frater and western range, with the permanent
outer buildings and the rest of the church, were not finished till
later. At Meaux a temporary two-storied building, church above
and dorter below, was used for some years until permanent buildings
were ready.

number of altars was necessary, so that brethren in holy orders might have frequent opportunities of celebrating mass. (3) Arrangements had to be made for processions, and especially for the procession before high mass on Sundays, which began and ended in the church and made the round of the claustral buildings.

§ 30. The result of these common requirements was the general prevalence of the cruciform plan in churches of monks and canons. The eastern arm contained the high altar and presbytery. The quire occupied the crossing of the transepts and one or more of the eastern bays of the nave. The transepts were provided with eastern chapels, and in the transept next the cloister direct access was given to the dorter by the night-stair, which was used by the convent in going to and returning from the night office of matins and lauds. The quire was separated from the rest of the nave by a stone screen with a loft above, known as the *pulpitum*, a bay west of which came another screen, the rood-screen. The nave usually had north and south aisles. In the aisle-wall next the cloister were two doorways, one opening into the east, the other into the west walk of the cloister. The Sunday procession left the church by the eastern doorway, which was also the entrance used by the convent for the day offices, and returned by the western. There was frequently a tower above the crossing, and the larger churches had additional towers at the west end of the aisles. Even Cistercian churches, in defiance of the statutes, succumbed in the later middle ages to the attractions of tower-building. A tower was built above the crossing at Kirkstall and at the west end of the nave at Furness. At Fountains, after a futile attempt to build above the crossing, the tower was added to the end of the north transept.

§ 31. The eastern arm of a Benedictine church was normally aisled. In the common plan of a Norman abbey church the presbytery ended in an apse, which contained the high altar, standing clear of the eastern wall, and projected a bay east of the ends of the aisles, which were internally apsidal but externally were finished off square. This plan was followed in Lanfranc's church at Canterbury, at Durham, Peterborough, Westminster and elsewhere, and was not confined to monastic churches. In England, however, a plan was sometimes followed which was unusual in Normandy, although it is common in Romanesque churches in other parts of France. The aisles in this case were continued round the apse, so as to form a processional path behind the altar ; and out of this path opened three apsidal chapels, as at Gloucester and Norwich, or five, as in the Cluniac church of Lewes, where the plan was borrowed from the parent church of Cluny. This plan was of great convenience for processions and afforded room for at least one additional altar. It was adopted in the abbey church of St Augustine at Canterbury, and in the rebuilding of the eastern arm of the neighbouring cathedral priory. Gloucester, Norwich and Tewkesbury are examples of its use in Benedictine churches; and it occurs in the Augustinian priory church of St Bartholomew, Smithfield. In these cases the processional path was retained through all later alterations, and the original arrangement is still quite clear; while the alternative and at one time more common plan has generally disappeared in England, and Peterborough is the one large church in which there are substantial remains of it above the foundations. Although the influence of Cluny upon foreign Romanesque architecture was considerable, the English Cluniac churches had no distinct plan of their own. Castle Acre, for example, followed the ordinary Norman plan as seen at Durham and Peterborough; and later developments at Castle Acre and Wenlock were carried out on models common to churches of other orders.

§ 32. The presbytery or space west of the altar in churches of the Norman period varied in length from two bays to four. At its west end a step (*gradus presbyterii*) divided it from the quire, which, as already noted, occupied the length of the crossing and the eastern bay or bays of the nave. The quire was an oblong enclosure cut off from the nave, aisles and transepts by screens on three sides, against which the stalls of the convent were arranged. It had three doorways. The western entrance, in the middle of the *pulpitum* or quire screen, was called the lower entry (*introitus inferior*). The upper entries (*introitus superiores*) or quire-doors (*ostia chori*) were lateral entrances in the screens next the transepts, on either side of the presbytery step, and were the way by which the convent came into quire. When the Sunday procession left the high altar, it passed out of the quire by the upper entry on the side furthest from the cloister, and returned, after making the circuit of the church and cloister-buildings, through the lower entry in the *pulpitum*. The stalls in the quire were occupied according to seniority. In an abbey church, the abbot sat against the western screen, on the south side of the lower entry, while the prior sat in the corresponding stall on the north. Where a prior was head of the house, he sat in the southern stall and the sub-prior in the northern. In the middle of the quire was the lectern, where, as at Durham, 'the Moncks did singe ther Legends at Mattins and other tymes.' On certain festivals, the epistle and gospel were chanted from the *pulpitum* at the west end of the quire. In these general arrangements, allowing for the divergences in the ritual of the various orders, there was very little difference between the interior of a monastic quire and that of

a church of secular canons. Where medieval stall-
work remains, as at Winchester and Chester, or in
the collegiate quires of Lincoln, Beverley, and Ripon,
the similarity is at once apparent; but monastic
quires were effectually isolated from the nave by the
rood-screen west of the *pulpitum*, an arrangement
which, though not unknown, was very rare in collegiate
churches.

§ 33. On leaving the quire by one of the upper
entries, the Sunday procession first visited the altars
in the transept on that side, and, while the celebrant
sprinkled each with holy water, anthems were sung
by the convent. The transept-chapels varied in
number. In the great abbey churches of the Norman
period, as at Norwich, Gloucester and Tewkesbury, a
single apsidal chapel projected from the east wall of
either transept. In churches with short presbyteries,
such chapels formed an effective group with the apse
and its chapels. Thus at St Mary's, York, and
St Albans, where the plan of the eastern apse without
a processional path was followed, the apse, projecting
beyond the rest of the church, was flanked on either
side by a row of three chapels, of which two opened
out of the transept; and of these two, the inner one,
nearest the aisle, projected further east than the
outer. At Durham, Ely and Peterborough, the
transepts were provided with eastern aisles, divided
by low screens or perpeyn walls into three chapels on

either side.   There were thus in the plan of these
three churches, eight altars in the transepts and
presbytery aisles: at St Mary's, York, and St Albans
there were six: at Westminster four; while at
Norwich, Gloucester and Tewkesbury, where there
was a processional path round the high altar, there
were five.

§ 34. The lengthening of the eastern limbs of
monastic churches, of which an early example was
the enlargement of Canterbury cathedral, completed
in 1130, provided additional chapels and a clear
course for the procession at the back of the high
altar.   At Canterbury, the new eastern limb was as
long as the nave and crossing together: the quire was
moved into its western part, and additional transepts,
each containing two chapels, were thrown out on
either side of the new presbytery, while three chapels
opened out of the processional path which encircled
the apse.   In this plan the night-entry was a doorway
in the eastern transept.   In the second rebuilding,
some fifty years later, the plan was lengthened further
to include a chapel for the shrine of St Thomas between the high altar and the ambulatory.   Although
in several cases, with the lengthening of the eastern
limb, the quire was transferred to a position east of
the transepts, this alteration was by no means general.
In the thirteenth century rebuilding at Westminster,
the high altar, presbytery and quire remained in their

old places, and the additional space in the new apse was devoted to the chapel and shrine of St Edward. The plans of Canterbury and Westminster were both elaborate versions of the Norwich and Gloucester plan. But, while this type of plan prevailed in the great churches of France, the plan which was preferred in England from the beginning of the thirteenth century onward was a long rectangular eastern limb. At Winchester and St Albans, the longest of our great churches, the quire did not extend east of the transepts, and the presbytery and high altar occupied their relative positions as in the older plan. Behind the screen or reredos of the high altar a bay was screened off as a feretory or shrine for the local saint. At this point the high roof of the church ceased, and the roof of the eastward extension was on a level with that of the aisles, which were thus returned to afford a processional path at the back of the feretory. On the east side of the processional path were chapels enclosed by screens, while a long aisleless Lady chapel was built out from the centre of the east wall. At Chester the eastern chapel, which contained St Werburgh's shrine, is directly at the back of the high altar, and no space was left for a processional path: this was remedied to some extent in the fifteenth century by prolonging the north aisle eastwards and so affording a lateral entrance to the chapel. In the east and north of England, as at Ely and Selby, it was customary

T. E. M.   4

Fig. 2. Croyland abbey: rood-screen and nave from S.E.

to continue the high roof to the extreme east end of
the church, and to prolong the aisles to the same
length on either side, so that externally the ambulatory
and eastern chapels are not definitely expressed. In
such cases a row of altars, divided by screens or perpeyn
walls, stood side by side against the east wall. These
alternative plans were not peculiar to the religious
orders, and the second plan was freely used in the
larger Yorkshire churches, by secular canons at York
and Ripon, by Benedictines at Selby, Whitby and
St Mary's, York, by Cistercians at Jervaulx and
Rievaulx, and by Augustinian canons at Guisbrough
and Kirkham.

§ 35. The Sunday procession, after making stations
at each of the eastern chapels in turn, came down the
aisle into the transept next the cloister, and, having
visited the altars there, passed into the cloister through
the eastern processional doorway in the nave. It
returned through the western processional doorway.
If, as at Durham, there was a chapel at the west end
of the church, the procession would enter it by the
doorway at the end of one aisle, and leave it by the
other. The western chapel at Durham, as at Glastonbury, was the Lady chapel. It was known at Durham
as the Galilee because the celebrant, entering it in
front of the convent at the end of the procession on
Sunday, the feast of the Resurrection, symbolised our
Lord going before His disciples into Galilee. The

name Galilee was also applied, as at Ely, or in the
Cistercian churches of Byland and Fountains, to
porches in front of the western doorway of a church.
The final station of the procession was in the middle
of the nave before the rood-screen.   Here the convent
stood in two long rows, the position of each member
being regulated by stones inserted in the floor of the
nave at equal intervals: such stones still remain beneath the grass at Fountains, and are known to have
existed elsewhere. Meanwhile, the celebrant sprinkled
the chief nave altar, which stood against the middle
of the screen, and was at Durham enclosed at the sides
and in front by wooden screens, which formed a chapel
or 'porch.'   On either side of the altar was a doorway through the screen, above which was the great
rood or crucifix, with a figure of St Mary on one side
and St John on the other: at Durham there were
also figures of archangels.   The rood-screen was
flanked by screens across the aisles, so that the
western part of the nave was entirely shut off from
the quire and from the eastern processional doorway.
The eastern part of the south aisle at Durham was
screened off as a chantry chapel, and there were also
two enclosed chapels further west, beneath opposite
arches of the nave, one of which was visited on the
way to the Galilee, and the other in returning.
There was frequently, as at St Albans, a row of
chapels beneath the arches, while in some cases,

as at Ely and Peterborough, where the nave projected some distance west of the cloister, more altars were provided in a transept at the west end. After the station at the rood altar and its neighbouring chapels had been concluded, the convent passed through the two doorways in the rood-screen, and, reuniting in the bay beyond, entered the quire through the doorway in the middle of the *pulpitum*. In many churches, as at Norwich, the *pulpitum* was formed by two parallel stone screens carrying the loft and occupying a bay of the nave. At Malmesbury it enclosed the bay west of the crossing, and its eastern screen is the reredos of the present parish altar. At Durham and Canterbury, where the quire was east of the crossing, the *pulpitum* was between the eastern piers, the rood-screen between the western. At Canterbury the eastern processional doorway was in the west wall of the transept next the cloister. At Durham it is in the usual position, but covered by a vestibule formed by placing the screen at the end of the south aisle one bay west of the rood-screen. The rood-screens at Croyland and at Tynemouth priory still remain among the ruins. At St Albans the *pulpitum* is gone, but the stone rood-screen remains; while at Blyth priory the place of the rood-screen was taken by a wall the whole height of the nave.

§ 36. Lay-folk were permitted to enter the naves

of monastic churches; and, even in Cistercian churches, where the whole building was strictly devoted to the uses of the monastery, doorways are sometimes found, as at Kirkstall, which may have been made for this purpose. In a large number of Benedictine and Augustinian churches, though by no means in the majority, an altar in the nave was appropriated to parochial services, and was served by a secular vicar or a curate appointed by the convent. The lay-folk entered the church by a doorway in the aisle opposite the cloister: the great western doorway was used only on special occasions, as in the procession on Palm Sunday or at an episcopal visitation. Sometimes, as at Blyth and Leominster, a special addition of an aisle or a second nave and aisle was made to the original nave, for the sake of parochial services. Such services, however, frequently interfered with the monastic offices, especially if the convent was singing one thing and the parishioners another. At Wymondham in Norfolk a dispute about the use of the bells by the parish led to a serious quarrel in the fifteenth century. The parishioners fastened up the rood-screen doors and appropriated the nave, and the dispute was healed only by the building of a separate bell-tower for the parish at the west end of the church. The monks of Rochester and the canons of Holy Trinity, Aldgate, built churches within their outer precincts for the parishioners whose services interfered

with their own. This arrangement, like that by which
the pairs of parish churches at Coventry, Evesham
and Bury St Edmunds were distinct from the monastery churches hard by, put an end to such constant
wrangling as occurred between monks and lay-folk
over the use of the south transept at Chester.

§ 37. Cistercian churches developed a special
plan of their own in keeping with the austere ideals
of their order. Some of their earliest churches, as at
Waverley and Tintern, had aisleless naves, short
transepts, each with one rectangular chapel upon its
eastern side and an aisleless rectangular presbytery.
This is a simple form of the normal Cistercian plan,
which, with its complement of aisles, appeared early
at Rievaulx, and may be seen to perfection at
Kirkstall and Buildwas. The presbytery, aisleless
and rectangular, projected some two bays east
of the crossing, the high altar being placed
slightly in advance of the east wall. The western
bay of the presbytery was covered on either side by
two or three rectangular chapels ranged along the
east side of the transepts, divided from each other by
solid walling, but with a continuous eastern wall.
The nave was aisled. The quire was in the usual
position, in the crossing and the eastern bays of the
nave, and was enclosed on north and south by stone
walls which were built flush with the inner faces of
the columns and across the length of the crossing.

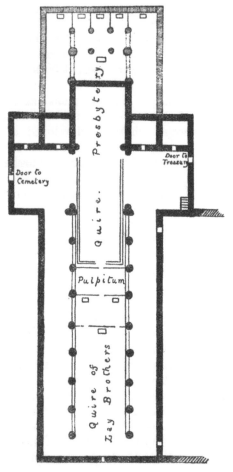

Fig. 3. Plan of typical Cistercian church, shewing
original form and later eastern enlargement.

The lower entry of the quire was, as usual, in the
middle of the *pulpitum*: the upper entries were
doors in the side-walls close to the presbytery.

§ 38. Such a plan obviously gave little scope for
processions, while the number of altars was limited
by the aisleless presbytery. While some churches,
such as Buildwas and Kirkstall, kept their early plan
without alteration, and while thirteenth-century
churches such as those of Sweetheart abbey in Kirk-
cudbrightshire and Valle Crucis in Wales were built
on the traditional plan, others were rebuilt with aisled
presbyteries and ranges of eastern chapels. In two
instances, at Croxden and in the extension of Hayles
made in 1271–7, the ordinary French Gothic plan of
an apse with a processional path and apsidal eastern
chapels was adopted. Special Cistercian models,
however, were provided by the rebuildings at Clairvaux (1174) and Cîteaux (1193). At Clairvaux an
apse took the place of the rectangular presbytery: the
east walls of the chapels next the presbytery were
removed, and these chapels were continued round
the apse as a processional path, out of which opened
a series of chapels, one from each bay, divided by
walls and covered by a common lean-to roof. The
plan of Cîteaux was simply a rectangular version of
that of Clairvaux: the presbytery was aisled, the aisles
were returned across the east end, and all three sides
surrounded by similar chapels walled off from each

other. Of the Clairvaux plan the only known example
in England is the thirteenth-century church of Beaulieu. The Cîteaux plan in a modified form was more
general. It is well seen at Dore, where there are no
chapels opening from the north and south aisles, but
the processional path has an eastern aisle containing
five chapels, originally divided from one another by
perpeyn walls. This plan was followed in the earlier
church at Hayles (1249–51), before the eastern arm
was extended to include the chapel of the Holy Blood.
In some churches, as at Byland and Waverley, the
processional path was provided by moving the high
altar a bay west of the main east wall, and placing
the chapels in the returned aisle, instead of building a
special aisle for them beyond. On the other hand, the
eastern limbs at Jervaulx, Rievaulx, Tintern, and
elsewhere were rebuilt in the thirteenth century upon
the ordinary aisled rectangular plan. The high altar
was placed two bays west of the east end: the processional path was in the bay between it and the
eastern chapels, which were ranged against the east
wall. The presbyteries in these churches were usually
walled off from the aisles, as may be seen in Tintern:
the walls were provided for from the beginning and
were sometimes bonded into the piers. As a rule,
such aisled presbyteries were short. Four bays was
a usual length, as at Jervaulx, Netley and Tintern:
this allowed two bays for the high altar and presbytery,

and the quire was left in its normal position. But at Rievaulx the eastern arm was lengthened to seven bays and included the quire. The thirteenth-century enlargement at Fountains gave four bays to the altar and presbytery, without removing the quire; while behind the altar was built a vast eastern transept two bays deep, with nine chapels against its east wall and a processional path in the western bay. This unusual and beautiful plan was imitated with great splendour in the Benedictine church of Durham.

§ 39. The chief peculiarity of the Cistercian transept was the arrangement, already described, of its eastern chapels. This was modified in later times, as at Furness, where the vaulting of the chapels was removed and replaced by a wooden roof at a higher level, and screen-walls took the place of the solid divisions. The night-stair from the monks' dorter was very generally placed against the west wall of the adjacent transept; while in the end wall of the opposite transept was the doorway through which funerals passed to the graveyard. At Furness, where the church, by an exceptional arrangement, stands between the greater part of the *curia* and the cloister, this doorway formed the main entrance to the church and was covered by a porch. Beaulieu, like Cîteaux, has the unusual feature of a western aisle in the transept opposite the cloister. Such aisles, though sometimes found in both transepts of

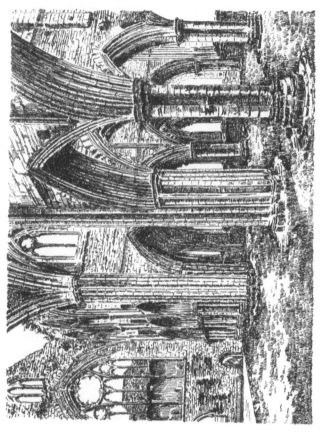

Fig. 4.   Tintern abbey: north transept and presbytery, shewing doorways to dorter and sacristy.

Benedictine churches, are rare in the churches of
Cistercians.

§ 40. Cistercian naves were not affected by the
problem of parochial services, but served special
purposes required by the peculiar constitution of the
order. So far as the Sunday procession was concerned,
their arrangements did not greatly vary from those of
other monasteries, although the position of the western
processional doorway with regard to the cloister was
rather different. The west end of the quire was shut
off by the *pulpitum*, which in the longer naves, as at
Fountains, consisted of two parallel screens with a
loft above, occupying a full bay, but was often a single
screen-wall with a loft. Against the west face of the
pulpitum there were two altars, one on each side of
the middle doorway. The bay west of these was
called the retro-quire, where infirm and aged monks
attended service, and was shut off on the west by the
rood-screen. This was of the usual character, with
an altar against its western face between two doorways. The nave west of the rood-screen was used as
the quire of the lay brothers, who had a night-stair
from their dorter in the adjacent aisle, and used the
western processional doorway as their day-entrance.
Their stalls were set against the walls which, as in
the presbytery, shut the nave off from its aisles :
these were discontinued in the westernmost bay, so as
to give a clear entry for the lay brothers and for

processions. This arrangement can be well seen at Tintern, where only the west bay on the north side, next the cloister, was left unwalled. The plan received its fullest extension at Fountains, where the nave was eleven bays long, of which seven were west of the rood-screen, while of the rest one was devoted to the quire, and one each to the *pulpitum*, the altars in front of it and to the retro-quire. At Furness, where there were ten bays, two were given to the quire, five were west of the rood-screen and the intermediate three were divided as at Fountains. In shorter churches, such as Buildwas (seven bays) and Tintern (six) some economy of space between the screens had to be studied. Thus, of eight bays at Kirkstall two were in the quire, four were west of the rood-screen, the *pulpitum* occupied a whole bay, and the remaining bay contained the altars on its western side : the space beneath the *pulpitum* may in this case have been used as a retro-quire. The *pulpitum* at Valle Crucis was a single screen-wall between the western piers of the crossing, and the quire did not extend into the short nave. After the lay brethren had ceased to be a part of Cistercian convents, the walls dividing their quires from the nave-aisles were removed where they were not in bond with the piers, and chapels were then made in the eastern bays of the aisles. Recent excavations at Rievaulx show this clearly. There is no trace of any new chapels at Furness, but there was probably always an altar there in each of the aisles, in a line with the altars next the *pulpitum*.

§ 41. The preference for a rectangular chancel, in our larger churches at any rate, may be attributed in some measure to the architectural influence exercised by the Cistercian order. It is certainly possible to trace Cistercian influence in some of the churches of canons regular. It cannot be said that churches of Augustinian canons followed any definite or uniform plan. Some, like St Bartholomew's, Smithfield, preferred plans for which the best contemporary models were Benedictine. But the plan of the first church at Haughmond was very like the early plans of Waverley and Tintern ; and when this was superseded by a larger church with its longer axis further north than before, the new presbytery was still aisleless and was still walled off from the transept-chapels immediately adjoining. Of these there were two on either side, both rectangular in shape, and those next the presbytery were longer than those on the outside. The same plan of presbytery and transept-chapels is found at Lilleshall, and is known to have existed at Fountains before the presbytery was aisled. Similarly the plan of presbytery and transepts at Bolton and Brinkburn is distinctly Cistercian in origin, and, when the presbytery at Bolton was lengthened in the fourteenth century, its aisleless form was retained. In Premonstratensian churches the likeness to the normal

Cistercian plan is often obvious. The original plan
of the eastern portion of the church at St Agatha's
was almost the same as that of Kirkstall; while the
plan of the same part of Torre is virtually identical
with those of Buildwas and Roche. As at Bolton,
the aisleless presbytery at St Agatha's was pro-
longed in the fourteenth century to twice its original
length.

§ 42. The plan of Haughmond and Lilleshall,
in which the presbytery walls remained unpierced,
while they were flanked with aisle-like chapels, is
found in some Premonstratensian churches, as at
Dale. At West Langdon the chapels were continued
the whole length of the presbytery. Usually, however, they stopped short of the east end. The
aisleless projection thus formed might contain, as
at Alnwick, the high altar. But at St Radegund's
near Dover, the eastern bay was the Lady chapel,
and between it and the high altar was a space for
processions, entered by doorways in the walls which
divided it from the aisles and in the screen on either
side of the high altar. In many Augustinian churches
a further development of this plan is found, in which
the chapels are real aisles, divided by arcades from
the presbytery, as at Cartmel and Lanercost, and the
eastern arm is so lengthened as to include the quire
or a portion of it. At St Frideswide's, Oxford (now
Christ Church cathedral), Repton and Dorchester,

where the plans are somewhat complicated by the addition of one or more extra chapels on one side, the high altar was, as at Cartmel and Lanercost, in the eastern bay, and the procession in going from one aisle to another had to pass in front of it. The aisled portion, however, was sometimes planned, as at Bristol, to include the quire and presbytery and a bay for the processional path behind the high altar: this was also the plan of the church of secular canons at Southwell. The eastern limb of Christchurch, Hants, is similar in plan to that of Bristol; but here the high roof stopped above the altar, and the roofs of the processional path and Lady chapel, as at Winchester, are on a level with those of the aisles, while above them is an upper story or loft, formerly the chapel of St Michael. The ground-plan of the Cluniac church of Castle Acre was enlarged on the lines followed at Cartmel and Lanercost: that of Wenlock approximated to those followed at Bristol and Christchurch. Variations of these types of plan are seen in the thirteenth-century enlargements of the Benedictine churches of Rochester and Worcester, in which the quires were placed in the eastern arm. Both churches have eastern transepts, and in both cases the high vault was continued to the end of an aisleless eastern projection, in which the high altar stood at Rochester with a clear space behind it. At Worcester the aisleless bay was the

Lady chapel, and the high altar stood west of the processional path.

§ 43. The naves of the larger churches of canons, such as Bridlington, Guisbrough and Worksop, were provided with their full complement of aisles. Christchurch and St Botolph's at Colchester are conspicuous instances of Augustinian conventual naves which were aisled in the twelfth century. But it is also certain that many canons' churches, like Haughmond, had no aisles to begin with. This, as we have seen, was a point in common between them and some early Cistercian churches. The nave at Lilleshall was never provided with aisles : the same thing happened at Kirkham, where the eastern arm was fully aisled in the thirteenth century. In such cases, where a nave had been originally planned without aisles, no aisle could be added on the side next the cloister without contracting the cloister or necessitating its rebuilding. Consequently aisleless naves were left as they were or were enlarged by an aisle only on the side which admitted of extension, opposite the church. The nave with a single aisle, although it is found in some Benedictine churches, as at the priories of Abergavenny and Bromfield, is certainly characteristic of churches of canons, and may be explained on these grounds. Among Augustinian examples are the churches of Bolton, Brinkburn, Canons Ashby, Haughmond, Hexham (as

planned in the thirteenth century), Lanercost, Newstead, Thurgarton and Ulverscroft: Dorchester, where
the broad south aisle is a westward continuation of
the original south transept, may be placed in the
same category.   Premonstratensian churches of the
type were Coverham, West Langdon, Shap and Torre.
It has been suggested that this partial addition of
aisles may have been caused by the canons' desire to
rival aisled Benedictine churches.   Large canons'
churches, however, such as those already mentioned, if
they were smaller than the great Benedictine churches,
were at any rate as completely planned ; and it is
probable that the enlargement of aisleless naves was
merely the result of the inconvenience of the cramped
space, especially where new altars were needed.   It
had nothing to do with the needs of parishioners :
only four out of the ten Augustinian, and none of the
Premonstratensian examples given above contained
parochial altars.   The enlargement was frequently
achieved, as at Canons Ashby and Thurgarton, with
a beautiful and perfectly unambitious effect.   At
Newstead, however, the builders, in projecting their
western façade, seem to have felt that the one-sided
plan hardly gave them an opportunity for the eleva-
tion they wanted; and so they disingenuously balanced
the west front of their north aisle by building out a
screen-wall, similar in design, against the west wall
of the cloister buildings.   This work, executed with

5—2

elaborate detail, shews that no funds can have been
wanting to build a south aisle, but that the sole
reason which prevented this was the inconvenience
which would have been caused to the cloister.

§ 44. The division of an aisleless nave by screens
is well illustrated at Lilleshall, where the bases of the
pulpitum and rood-screen both remain, and there
was a wall further west which screened the nave
from a vaulted vestibule, apparently planned as the
ground-floor of a tower. Examples of aisleless naves
are found in churches of all orders. Instances of
Benedictine churches, such as St Benet's, Hulme, in
Norfolk, are known, where this plan seems out of
keeping with the importance and wealth of the
convent. The Cluniac priory church of Bromholm
is another case from the same county. Salley, a
Cistercian church on the borders of Yorkshire and
Lancashire, had a fully aisled quire, but a very short
aisleless nave, which was little more than a vestibule
to the church and covered only the eastern part of
the north walk of the cloister. The nave of the
Scottish abbey of Kelso, which belonged to the order
of Thiron, has long been supposed to have been a mere
vestibule or *narthex*; but recent investigation seems
to prove that the character of the existing remains of
the church has been misinterpreted.

§ 45. An entirely aisleless plan, in which the church
was a mere parallelogram without transepts and

Fig. 5. Mount Grace priory: tower-arches and nave from N.E.

without an arch between presbytery and nave, is found
at the Cistercian abbey of Cymmer, near Dolgelly,
where, however, a short north aisle or chapel was built
later near the west end of the nave. Such a plan may
have been used in many small houses, where there
were only two or three brethren in priest's orders,
and very few altars were needed in addition to the
high altar. It was, in fact, the characteristic plan of
the churches of certain orders. (1) Nuns' churches,
such as Nun Monkton in Yorkshire, were very
generally planned as aisleless rectangles, for the
obvious reason that little more than one altar was
necessary. It is rare to find a nunnery church
planned on the scale of Romsey, with a full complement of aisles and transepts and a carefully contrived
processional path. Sometimes, as at Lacock, a chapel
was added to the church, but this was an excrescence
which did not conceal the character of the original
plan. (2) The ascetic Carthusian order preferred
this plan, which was adopted at Mount Grace. It
was modified, however, some years after the church
was built, by the insertion of a tower upon arches
between the presbytery and nave, west of which
transeptal chapels were built out from the nave walls
on either side. Still later, a long chapel, containing
two altars, was built at right angles to the south wall
of the presbytery. (3) The plans of friars' churches,
which frequently, as at Lynn and Richmond, had a

tower between the nave and presbytery, bear a strong
family likeness to that of Mount Grace ; and in some
cases, as at Brecon and at Hulne, near Alnwick, they
were without a structural division.   The naves, however, of some of their later town churches, where
large congregations attended the preaching of the
Dominican order, were built, as in the splendid
example at Norwich, with north and south aisles.
(4) It is evident that churches of Gilbertine canons,
as at Malton, sometimes followed an ordinary aisled
plan.   But in the double houses of the order, if
Watton is typical of the rest, the church was a long
aisleless building on one side of the nuns' cloister,
and was divided lengthways by a wall, the division
next the cloister being appropriated to the nuns, and
the outer division, which had its own doorway, to the
canons.   There was a doorway in the wall between
the two altars, which could be used for processions
and by the celebrant at the nuns' altar ; but the
seclusion of the two portions of the convent was
carefully maintained, and the holy-water and pax
were passed from the nuns' to the canons' quire
through a turn-table in the wall.   The canons also
had a chapel on the south side of their own cloister,
which was a simple aisleless rectangle.

CHAPTER III

THE CLOISTER AND ITS BUILDINGS

§ 46. The cloister (*claustrum*) was, as its name
implies, an enclosed space, surrounding all four sides
of a rectangular court. The four walks of the
cloister were roofed in: the walls next the court
were pierced at first with open arcades, and later
with large window-openings. One walk adjoined the
nave of the church, and part of the east walk was
overlapped by the adjacent transept. On the east
and the two remaining sides of the cloister were the
buildings necessary to the daily life of the convent,
the chapter-house being invariably at the back of the
east walk and the refectory or frater at the back of
the walk opposite the church. The entrance from the
outer court varied in position according to the site of
the monastery: in many houses, as at Torre, it was a
passage through or at one end of the western range,
but at Durham, Worcester and some of the larger
Benedictine houses it was a vaulted entry at the end
of the east walk furthest from the church. There
were, as we have seen, two doorways from the church,
of which the eastern was the ordinary entrance used
by the convent in the daytime. The Sunday procession left the church by this doorway, and passed along
the east walk; and, after visiting the chief buildings

on three sides of the cloister, returned into church by the doorway at the end of the west walk.

§ 47.   In all monasteries, save in those of the Carthusian order, the walk next the church was the ordinary place where the convent spent the hours of the day allotted to study and contemplation.   For this reason the cloister was normally planned on the south, the sunnier side of the church, where the high walls of nave and transept checked the north and east winds.   This walk, which was omitted from the route of the Sunday procession, was sometimes enclosed at either end by screens.   In early times the brethren seem to have sat side by side on the stone benches which, as at Worcester, were set against the church wall between the buttresses.   But at a later date the part of the walk next the court was divided by short partition walls into a number of small studies called carrels (*caroli*, i.e. enclosed spaces). At Durham, where the walk was ten bays long and was lighted by ten three-light windows, there were thirty carrels, three to each window.   The carrels remain at Gloucester, twenty in number, two to each of the ten four-light windows.   They were roofed at the level of the window-transoms, so that the upper portions of the windows gave plenty of light to the walk behind.   Each contained a desk for books : at Durham they were wainscoted, and entered by doors, the tops of which were pierced, so

Fig. 6. Gloucester: south walk of cloister with monks' carrels.

that each monk as he worked was under survey. As
private property was forbidden, no religious was
allowed to keep books of his own in his carrel.
Manuscripts in use were kept in special cupboards
or almeries (*armaria*), which at Durham were ranged
against the church wall. Such book-cupboards were
placed in the cloister where there was room for them.
At Worcester there are two in the east walk near the
chapter-house door, while at Gloucester the eastern-
most carrel and two small cupboards projecting into
the court from the east walk were probably used for
this purpose. In Cistercian houses a special place
was set aside for the library; but in the houses of
most orders no definite part of the plan was so distinguished, and it is not until a late date that, at
Canterbury and Durham, we hear of separate rooms
assigned to the library, as distinct from the cupboards
and presses in the cloister[1].

§ 48. In the ordinary Benedictine plan, which,
although subject to some variation, was the model,
founded on convenience, for the other monastic orders,
the eastern range of buildings had a ground-floor and
upper story, and projected some distance to the south
or north, as the case might be, beyond the cloister.

---

[1] At St Albans, where we have much information about the
library, two-thirds of the demesne tithes in Hatfield and some tithes
in Redbourn were assigned between 1077 and 1098 *ad volumina
ecclesiae* (i.e. the church-books) *facienda*.

The upper story was the dorter (*dormitorium*) of the convent, which normally was carried through the whole range as far as the transept of the church. On the ground-floor, the chapter-house, entered by a doorway near the middle of the east walk, was a long building which projected eastwards at right angles to the range. It was very frequently separated from the church, as at Durham and Worcester, by a vaulted passage which gave access to the graveyard at the east end of the church. This was the parlour (*locutorium*), where the rule of silence was relaxed and necessary conversation could be held. At Durham, it is said that merchants were allowed to bring their wares here for sale, but this seems to be a mistake for the outer parlour, which, as at Gloucester, was in the western range, and the eastern parlour was reserved for the convent. Occasionally, as at Rochester and Wenlock, the chapter-house joined the church without the intervening parlour: and at Westminster the place of the parlour was taken by the chapel of St Faith, the only entrance to which was from the south transept.

§ 49. The chapter-house (*domus capitularis*) was the place where, every day after prime, the convent met together for the confession and correction of faults and for the discussion of business concerning the house as a whole. At these meetings a chapter (*capitulum*) of the rule was read daily, and from this circumstance the name of chapter was transferred

both to the meeting and the building. Here too the
visitor of the monastery held his periodical inquiries,
prefaced by a sermon from one of his clerks or of the
senior members of the house. In the twelfth and
thirteenth centuries, as at Durham and Fountains,
the chapter-house was the customary burial-place for
abbots and other heads of houses. The dead bodies
of monks rested in the chapter-house at Durham, and
matins of the dead were sung for them here before
they took their last journey through the parlour to
the graveyard. The building was normally oblong
in shape, undivided by columns into aisles, and was
usually vaulted. At Durham, Gloucester and Reading
it ended in an apse. The abbot or prior occupied a
raised seat at the east end, with the principal officers
on his right and left. The rest of the convent sat on
stone benches round the walls; while near the centre
of the floor was the desk or lectern (*analogium*) from
which the daily lection from the martyrology and the
chapter for the day were read. The breadth of the
chapter-house generally corresponded to three bays
of the cloister, with a doorway in the middle of the
west wall and a window on either side.

§ 50. In most houses, as in the Augustinian abbey
of canons at Haughmond and of canonesses at Lacock,
the chapter-house roof was on a level with that of
the cloister, to allow of the continuation of the dorter
or of a passage from the dorter to the transept across

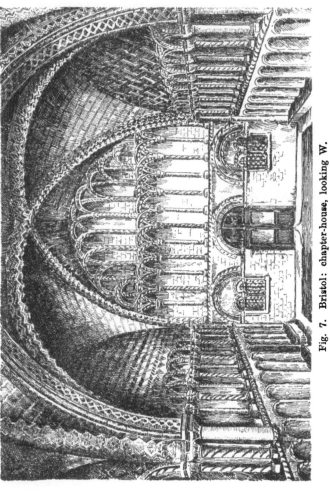

Fig. 7. Bristol: chapter-house, looking W.

its western end. But in the larger houses, especially
of the Benedictines, it was often an aisleless hall
occupying the whole height of the range. Where, as
at Canterbury, Gloucester and Reading, it was of this
type and opened directly from the cloister, the dorter
was obviously shut off from direct communication
with the church. But at Bristol, Chester, Westminster and elsewhere, the lofty chapter-houses stood
entirely at the back of the eastern range, and the
dorter was carried across a vaulted vestibule, which
was divided by columns into three or, at Westminster,
into two alleys, and was either open to the cloister,
as at Bristol, or, as at Chester, was entered by a
doorway with a window on either side, like the doorway of the chapter-house beyond. It has been said
that the chapter-house was usually planned without
aisles: this was the case in the larger Benedictine
houses, and in such houses of moderate size as
Haughmond, the Premonstratensian abbey of Dry-
burgh in Scotland, or the Benedictine nunnery of
St Radegund at Cambridge. But the Cistercian
order preferred chapter-houses divided into alleys
by rows of columns, and the influence of their
beautiful buildings may be seen in the aisled chapter-
houses of Lacock or of the Premonstratensian abbey
of Beeleigh. Nor was the chapter-house always
oblong. Apsidal examples have been given; and,
when that at Gloucester was rebuilt in the fifteenth

century, it was finished with a three-sided apse.
There are also circular and polygonal chapter-houses.
At Worcester the twelfth-century chapter-house is a
circular building, entered directly from the cloister,
and vaulted from a central column. In the fifteenth
century, when the abutments shewed signs of giving
way, it was remodelled externally into a ten-sided
polygon. No vestibule was necessary here, as the
dorter was placed in another part of the cloister, and
more room could accordingly be given to the chapter-
house. At Dore, the chapter-house was polygonal; at
Margam it was internally circular, externally twelve-
sided. The Benedictine chapter-house at Evesham
was ten-sided. Between 1245 and 1250 was built
the octagonal chapter-house of Westminster, the
prototype of the secular buildings at Salisbury
and Wells, raised upon an undercroft and divided
from the cloister by a long vestibule; and there were
octagonal chapter-houses in the Augustinian priories of
Bolton and Carlisle. The most peculiar plan was that of
the twelfth-century Premonstratensian chapter-house
at Alnwick, where a rectangular western vestibule was
combined with a circular eastern portion of the same
height, roofed in one span without a central column.

§ 51. Where the infirmary buildings stood due
east of the cloister, as at Canterbury, they were
approached by a passage through the east range,
next the chapter-house. Their position, however,

was variable; and in such instances the infirmary
passage represented a bay cut off from the vaulted
undercroft of the dorter, which formed the rest of the
ground-floor of the eastern range. At Westminster,
where this sub-vault belongs to the earliest portion
of the monastery, the ordinary custom was followed
of dividing it into two apartments. The northern
and smaller, occupying the two bays at the south end
of the east walk, was the treasury, known at Westminster as the chapel of the Pyx, because the
currency, contained in a box or casket (*pyxis*) was
brought there for trial. The southern division extended for five bays beyond the cloister, and was the
common house or warming-house (*calefactorium*),
which contained the fireplace where the monks
warmed themselves in winter. In Cluniac monasteries
this was also the bleeding-house of the monks. If,
however, the Westminster arrangement may be quoted
as typical, it was not invariable. The customary position for the warming-house was beneath the dorter;
and consequently, if the dorter, as sometimes happened,
occupied an abnormal situation, the warming-house
followed suit. Thus, on the contracted site at Gloucester, the dorter was on the first floor of a building
at right angles to the cloister, parallel to the chapter-
house. At Worcester, it was at right angles to
the west walk of the cloister. Probably the early
plan at Durham was like that at Westminster, but

eventually the dorter and common house were removed
to the west range. The plan of St Agatha's, which
in more than one respect resembles that of Durham,
also shews the dorter and common house in the west
range; but, while the treasury at Durham was the
part of the dorter sub-vault between the common
house and the church, the treasury at St Agatha's, as in
many canons' houses, was probably the sacristy in the
east range, between the church and chapter-house,
where at Durham we find the parlour. The dorter
and common house at Canterbury were in the usual
place ; but the treasury was in quite a different part
of the monastery, between the infirmary and one of
the chapels of the apse ; and at Gloucester, at any
rate after the fourteenth century, the treasury was a
first-floor room above the monks' parlour, between
the chapter-house and north transept[1].

§ 52. The dorter generally communicated with
the transept of the church by the night-stair, of
which a splendid example remains at Hexham, the
head of the stair being divided from the dorter by
a lobby or a room over the parlour. Even where, as
at Haughmond, the dorter did not extend over the
chapter-house, there was sometimes a passage or

---

[1] At Evesham two of the obedientiaries' checkers or offices were
in the sub-vault of the dorter. Here also was the misericord, which
had a door into the infirmary garden. The bleeding-house was a
vaulted room beneath the rere-dorter.

gallery which led from it to the transept. There was always a day-stair to the dorter from the cloister, the ordinary position for which, as at Westminster, was between the chapter-house or its vestibule and the treasury or the common house; and when, as in examples already cited, the chapter-house entirely cut off the dorter from the church, this stair would be used for the night-services as well as for ordinary access in the daytime. In such cases, the entrance to the church was through the eastern processional doorway, but at Canterbury the monks, on their way from the dorter to the night-service, passed through a gallery on the first floor of the eastern or infirmary cloister to the doorway in the north-eastern tran-sept. In smaller monasteries there was often some difficulty in fitting the day-stair into the plan of the eastern range. In the Premonstratensian house of St Radegund the day-stair was a straight flight of steps from the lobby between the dorter and the church wall, at the other end of which was a turret containing the night-stair. At Lacock there was a single stair next the church, parallel with the east walk and dividing it from the large sacristy which filled the space between the church and chapter-house.

§ 53. Wainscot partitions divided the dorter in-ternally into a series of cubicles with a passage down the centre. Each cubicle was lighted by a window, and at Durham each contained a desk at which monks could work, if, as for example at the mid-day *siesta* in summer, they were unable to go to sleep. This was the ordinary late arrangement: it is probable that in early monasteries the beds stood against the wall between the windows without any partitions. Although several monastic dorters are still roofed, as at Westminster and Durham, where they are in use as chapter libraries, at the Cistercian abbeys of Cleeve, Ford (where the dorter is now divided into many small rooms) and Valle Crucis, and at the Premonstratensian abbey of Beeleigh, the internal partitions have disappeared. At the further end of the dorter or at right angles to the further wall from the cloister, there was always a building known as *domus necessaria, necessarium,* or in English the rere-dorter, which was a long gallery with a row of seats against one wall, each lighted by a window and divided by a partition from the next. Beneath the seats was a drain or running stream, above which the partitions were carried by transverse arches: on the ground-floor the drain was shut off by a wall from the vaulted undercroft of the gallery. The *necessarium* at Canterbury, known as the third dorter, was 145 feet long: it opened from the north-east corner of the great dorter, and was at right angles to the east wall, parallel to the second dorter, in which the obedientiaries or officers of the house slept. It contained 55 seats at first, 50 later. At Lewes the later *necessarium*, a separate building on lower ground than the dorter and connected with it by a bridge and stair, was 158 feet long and contained 66 seats. At Furness the *necessarium* stood east of the dorter and parallel to it, with a two-storied building connecting the two. Here the seats were arranged back to back against a middle wall, with a passage at either side.

§ 54. In the monasteries of all orders, the Cistercian order alone excepted, the range of buildings opposite the church, uniting the eastern and western cloister-buildings, had its major axis parallel with that of the church, and was entered by a doorway from the cloister near its west end. There was often at its east end a vaulted passage through the range, which continued the east walk of the cloister, and led either, as at Durham, into the outer court, or, as at Gloucester and Peterborough, to the infirmary buildings, and from this passage or 'dark cloister' at Westminster the common house beneath the dorter was entered. The larger part of the range was devoted to the frater or dining-hall of the monastery (*refectorium*). In several cases, the frater was raised upon a cellar, which was in many such instances, as at Gloucester, the great cellar and buttery of the house. Where such cellars existed, a stair led up through the frater doorway to the west end of the hall, which, as

in ordinary houses, was partitioned off from the rest
by screens.   The screens, entered on the level where
there was no cellar, formed a passage to the kitchen at
the back of the range, and had a pantry on the west
side.   This passage existed at Durham and St Agatha's,
where, above the pantry, the roof of which was of
course on a much lower level than that of the hall,
there was a loft, used in later days at Durham for
the daily meals of the monks, who used the frater
only on certain festivals, leaving it to the novices on
ordinary days.   The frater itself was an aisleless hall
with a wooden roof.   Across the east end was the
high table for the principal members of the convent:
the others sat at two or more tables set lengthways
in the body of the hall.   Near the high table, in the
wall opposite the cloister, was the pulpit, from which
a portion of Scripture or of some homily in Latin
was read by one of the brethren during meals.
A window-recess was generally enlarged to form the
pulpit, the floor and parapet of which were corbelled
out towards the hall: it was entered by a stair, as at
Chester or in the beautiful Cistercian example at
Beaulieu, in the thickness of the wall, with an open
arcade in its inner face.   There were also cupboards
and shelves in the frater for plate, linen and earthen-
ware.   In the Cistercian abbey of Cleeve there
remains above the high table a mural painting of
the Crucifixion : a similar painting was made in 1518

at Durham upon the upper part of the west wall.
At Worcester a sculptured figure of our Lord in
majesty occupies the middle of the east wall.

§ 55. The kitchen was, as has been said, external
to the cloister, though necessarily in close connexion
with the frater. In some of the greater houses, as at
Canterbury, Durham and Glastonbury, it was a detached building, which was rebuilt in the fourteenth
century on a square plan, with fireplaces in the
angles, the arches of which supported an octagonal
superstructure and vaulted roof, the smoke being
conveyed through flues to a central louvre. A passage
connected the kitchen with the frater and screens,
and at Durham food was served through an opening
in the frater wall called the dresser window. The
great kitchens of Durham and Glastonbury are still
entire. In the majority of cases, the kitchen was
probably a rectangular building ; and sometimes, as
at Lacock, it stood west of the frater, in the angle
between it and the western range. Here, where the
frater was upon an upper floor, the lobby at the foot
of the stair was the entrance to the kitchen, and the
fireplaces were in the outer walls.

§ 56. In the cloister, near the entrance to the
frater, was the lavatory (*lavatorium*), where the
brethren washed their hands before meals. In some
cases, as at Durham and Wenlock, an octagonal or
circular building, projecting into the cloister-garth

Fig. 8.   Worcester: lavatory in west walk of cloister.

opposite the frater doorway, contained a great laver, filled by taps from a pipe in a central pillar. Each monk could wash at his separate tap, the water from which fell into a basin at the foot of the laver and was carried away by a waste-pipe. The ingeniously contrived water-supply at Canterbury served three such laver-houses and a fourth laver in the so-called north hall[1]. The great laver-house in the infirmary cloister was used by monks on their way from the dorter to the night-office, when they entered the church through the eastern transept: this still remains, as well as the arches and the base of the trough of that near the frater. At Wenlock there remains a small apartment in the west wall of the south transept, close to the eastern processional doorway from the cloister, which may have been a lavatory for use before the night-office; but the theory that it was the library of the monastery is more likely. A more usual arrangement was not an isolated laver, but a trough fed by a pipe in the wall behind and emptied by a waste-pipe at one end. This is the form of which traces most commonly remain in cloisters, where the lavatory and its towel-cupboards

[1] Notices relating to water-supply are frequent in monastic chronicles. In 1216, when the old spring at Waverley dried up, a monk named Simon brought the waters of several springs by a culvert into a conduit which was called St Mary's fount. The new lavatory at Malmesbury was finished in 1284.

were placed in arched recesses either, as at Peterborough or in several Cistercian houses, in the wall
of the frater, or, as at Worcester, Haughmond and
Hexham, in the wall of the western range, not far
from the frater doorway. The lavatory at Gloucester,
on the trough principle, remains within a rectangular
building projecting from the wall opposite the frater
into the cloister-garth: the towel-cupboard was in
the north wall of the cloister next the frater. Towel-
cupboards also were formed by recesses in similar
positions in the south wall at Durham[1].

§ 57. The ground-floor of the western range of
buildings, as at Canterbury, Chester and Peterborough,
was usually the cellarer's building (*cellarium*), containing the great cellar and buttery of the monastery,
and frequently divided from the church by a vaulted
passage, which was the main entrance to the cloister
from the *curia* and was the outer parlour, where
necessary business could be done with lay-folk. But
the variable position of the *curia* with regard to the
cloister made the use of this range liable to variation;
and sometimes, as we have seen, the great cellar was
a vault beneath the frater. In two convents of women,
the Benedictine house of St Radegund at Cambridge
and the Augustinian house at Lacock, the ground-floor

---

[1] The weekly maundy (*mandatum*) or foot-washing took place at
the lavatory; the arrangement is well seen at Fountains, where the
monks sat on an upper ledge with their feet in the trough below.

was divided into separate rooms. The outer parlour
at Lacock was a passage near the centre of the
range : the rooms next the church may have been
used by the chaplains of the convent, while a large
room north of the passage may have been the guest-
hall where inferior visitors or pilgrims were enter-
tained by the cellaress. The upper floor probably
contained the abbess' lodging or *camera*, with her
guest-hall, in which visitors of the better class were
accommodated, above the cellaress' hall. It was at
any rate a very general custom, save in Cistercian
monasteries, for the upper floor to form part of the
abbot's or prior's separate lodging, and to contain his
guest-hall. Originally the head of the house slept in
the dorter with his brethren; but before the end of
the twelfth century he began to occupy separate
rooms, which in the larger monasteries developed
into a house of some size. At Peterborough the
abbot's lodging, now the bishop's palace, consisted of
a separate block of buildings standing to the west
of the *cellarium*, and entered from the outer court
through its own gatehouse. It was joined to the
cellarium by a wing, on the upper floor of which was
the abbot's solar or great chamber; and this communicated with the guest-hall on the first floor of the
cellarium, between which and the church, above the
outer parlour, was the abbot's chapel. The older
abbot's lodging at Gloucester, afterwards appropriated

to the prior, and now used as the deanery, was also separated by a small court from the cloister, and a wing next the church contained the abbot's chapel above the outer parlour; but here there was no western cloister range, and consequently the abbot's guest-hall was not within the claustral buildings. The archbishop's palace at Canterbury occupied practically the whole space west of the *cellarium*, with entrances to the cloister at both ends: the *curia* was on the north of the cloister, and the outer parlour was a passage between the west end of the frater and the cellarer's building.

§ 58. An important variation of plan in the western range occurs in three prominent instances. In each case the peculiarity is determined by the fact that a river forms the western boundary of the site, and afforded special convenience for drainage, while in two cases, at Durham and Worcester, the western range was on the side furthest from the town houses near the monastery. (1) At Worcester the cellarage was beneath the frater, and there was no western range parallel to the cloister. The dorter, with the common house below, was at right angles to the west walk of the cloister, and the rere-dorter was at the further end of this building next the river. A passage between the common house and the church led to the infirmary. (2) At Durham the older dorter and common house seem to have been, as at Peterborough,

Fig. 9. Durham: ceiling of dorter (now the chapter library).

in the eastern range and its southward extension,
next the chapter-house. But in the thirteenth century
a long range was built at the back of the west walk.
The great dorter occupied the whole of the upper
floor. Its southern end, which crossed the west end
of the frater range, was appropriated to the novices;
and a stair into the cloister, close to the church, at
the northern end, served for day and night use alike.
The vaulted ground-floor next the cloister was divided
into a treasury next the church and a common house.
In the bay at the junction of the south and west
walks a passage led through the range to the infirmary,
which, as at Worcester and for the same reasons, was
on the west side of the monastery. The bays beyond
this contained the cellar and buttery, now known as
the crypt, with entrances at one end from the infirmary and at the other from the cellarer's checker
or office and the kitchen buildings in the outer court.
A part of the old eastern range next the chapter-
house was used as a prison for refractory monks,
while the place of the rest was taken by the prior's
lodging, now part of the deanery. (3) In the Premonstratensian house of St Agatha, the dorter was on
the first floor of the western range and extended
southwards, as at Durham, across the west end of the
frater: its stair descended to the cloister at the south
end of the west walk, dividing the common house
and adjacent cellarage from the cellarer's guest-hall,

which formed the five southern bays of the dorter sub-vault. There was, however, a large two-storied annexe west of the dorter, the upper story of which seems to have been used for lodging guests of the better class, while, of the three divisions of its ground-floor, the middlemost and largest may have been occupied by their servants, with a narrow cellar on the east, and a drain, crossed by transverse arches, on the west side. The whole arrangement is quite exceptional and was probably unique; but the plan of the dorter sub-vault, allowing for some difference in use, bears a strong resemblance to the plan at Durham.

CHAPTER IV

THE CISTERCIAN CLOISTER

§ 59. Having thus traced the position of the various buildings in the normal cloister-plan, we may consider the features peculiar to cloisters of the Cistercian order—features for which the internal arrangement of their churches have in some degree prepared us. It has been pointed out by Mr Mickle-thwaite that the plan of the Cistercian cloister is indicated by the order in which the buildings are directed to be visited in the Sunday procession —viz. chapter-house, parlour, dorter, rere-dorter,

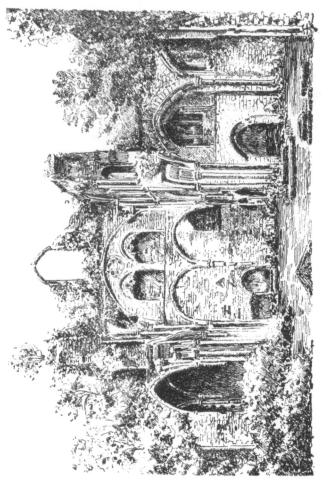

Fig. 10. Netley abbey : south transept and south aisle of nave, shewing doorways to sacristy and dorter, and eastern processional doorway.

warming-house, frater, kitchen, cellarer's building. It
will be observed that the parlour in this list comes between the chapter-house and dorter, and was therefore
on the further side of the chapter-house from the
church. On the other hand, although at Furness and
Waverley the chapter-house directly joins the south
transept of the church, there was in most Cistercian
houses an intervening building. The ground-floor of
this, however, was not a passage—for the way to the
graveyard was through the doorway in the opposite
transept—but was divided into two parts by a transverse wall. The eastern division, entered from the
transept, was a vestry (*vestiarium*): the western,
entered from the cloister, was probably the library
(*librarium*), outside which, in the west wall of the
transept, was the book-cupboard (*armarium com-
mune*), a wainscoted recess in which the books wanted
for constant use in cloister were kept. At Furness,
where the chapter-house was entered by a short
vestibule, the entrance-arch was flanked by two
similar arches, each of which opened into a rectangular
apartment: these rooms probably formed the library.
In the later middle ages the partition-wall between
the library and vestry was taken down at Fountains,
and the double chamber was converted into a passage.
The books appear to have been removed into closets
formed by enclosing the western bays of the north
and south alleys of the chapter-house.

§ 60. Lofty chapter-houses, like those of Gloucester
and Bristol, are not found in the Cistercian plan, in
which the dorter was almost invariably continued as
far as the church and was provided with an annexe
above the eastern projection of the chapter-house.
Furness is a case in which the chapter-house, as
already stated, had a vestibule ; but here the vestibule
is not a passage through the whole width of the
eastern range, but a porch, above which a gallery
was carried from the dorter to the night-stair.   The
roof of the chapter-house itself was somewhat higher,
but there was the usual room on the upper floor.
The chapter-house was usually an oblong, as at
Fountains, or, as at Furness, a nearly square building,
divided into alleys, generally three in number, by
rows of columns which supported vaulting.   The
entrance, in most cases, followed the customary plan
of a central doorway with a window on either side.
Vaulted chapter-houses may still be seen at Buildwas,
Kirkstall and Valle Crucis.   That at Buildwas is of
the normal plan, vaulted in three alleys.   At Kirkstall
the western part is vaulted in four alleys and has two
wide archways from the cloister, while the eastern
part beyond the range, rebuilt at the close of the
thirteenth century, is vaulted in two alleys.   The
Valle Crucis chapter-house is a fourteenth-century
rebuilding with the usual three alleys, but has a thick
west wall, in which, on the south side of the central

entrance, is the day-stair to the dorter, while on the north side is a vaulted book-cupboard, entered from the interior of the building. At Ford, where the chapter-house is now used as a private chapel, it is a vaulted building of the twelfth century, undivided by columns.

§ 61. The monks' parlour (*auditorium juxta capitulum*) was a narrow vaulted apartment in the ground-floor of the eastern range between the chapter-house and the sub-vault of the dorter. It was occasionally used, as at Beaulieu and Waverley, for a passage to the infirmary; but a separate passage, where the infirmary stood east of the range, was also made, as at Fountains, through the adjacent bay of the dorter sub-vault, which was walled off from the rest. The sub-vault, a long apartment, which at Furness extended no less than twelve bays south of the passage, was generally divided into two vaulted alleys by a central range of columns. It may have been partitioned off and applied to various uses, but at Furness it seems to have been undivided. From arrangements which are known to have existed at Clairvaux in 1517, it is now supposed to have been used, at any rate in part, as the house of the novices, possibly divided into a day-room, dorter and lodging for the novice-master. In a few instances, as at Croxden, Furness and Jervaulx, one or two of the southernmost bays originally formed an open *loggia*,

7—2

with piers and arches taking the place of the outer
walls: this space, however, in the two latter cases,
was walled in after no long time. It may be noted
that in the Benedictine houses of Peterborough and
Westminster, where the common house was, according
to the ordinary plan, in the sub-vault, a chapel was
built as an eastern annexe, which was probably used
at Peterborough as the chapel of the novices. This
appears to bring corroborative evidence to the pre-
vailing theory of the use of the Cistercian sub-vault,
of which no part, however, was employed as the
common or warming-house.

§ 62.   The Cistercian dorter and rere-dorter shew
no important variation from the habitual plan. The
position of the rere-dorter, at the end of the dorter
or at right angles to it, or, as at Furness, in a separate
building, was dictated by convenience for drainage.
The room above the chapter-house was sometimes
separate, as at Kirkstall and Valle Crucis, but was
open to the rest of the dorter at Buildwas and
Fountains. It may possibly have been appropriated
to the abbot in the first instance, and afterwards, like
the second dorter at Canterbury, may have been used
by the obedientiaries or by the prior. At Valle Crucis
the room contains a fireplace and is entered by
a passage on the north side, which also leads to a
small room next the church. Originally the day-stair
to the dorter was placed in the eastern range of

buildings, between the parlour and the dorter sub-vault: clear indications of this remain at Fountains and Kirkstall, and the day-stair is still in this position at Cleeve. But in most cases the stair was afterwards removed and placed against the west side of the sub-vault, between the eastern range and the range opposite the church, in the position which in Benedictine houses is generally occupied by a passage to the outer buildings. By a most unusual arrangement, the dorter at Waverley was on the ground-floor of the range, raised only by a few steps above the cloister. There was no upper floor, although a room between the dorter and parlour was divided into two stages[1]. The chapter-house was an undivided oblong building, vaulted in three bays; and there was, of course, no special night-entry to the church.

§ 63. The buildings connecting the east and west ranges of the Cistercian cloister were divided into three parts, with the warming-house on the east, the frater in the middle and the kitchen on the west, all entered from the cloister. It is probable that in the first instance the Cistercian frater was built in the usual way, with its major axis from east to west. This is the plan at Sibton in Suffolk and Merevale in Warwickshire: there are clear traces of it at Kirkstall, and evidences of foundations at Fountains. In the

---

[1] The upper stage was probably the treasury, which the account of the flood of 1265 shews to have been on an upper floor.

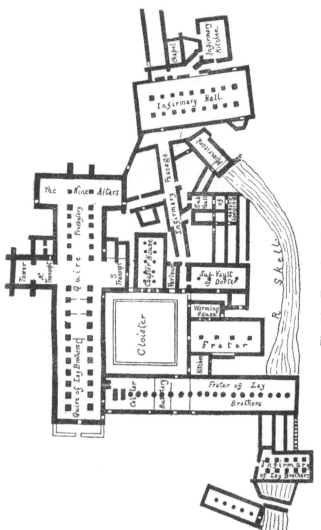

Fig. 11. Fountains abbey: plan.

Savigniac houses, afterwards Cistercian, the frater
seems to have been built from east to west, and at
Buckfast this position was apparently never altered.
But such fraters were cramped in size by their
position between the warming-house and kitchen,
and, before the end of the twelfth century they
were built or, as at Fountains and Kirkstall, rebuilt at right angles to the cloister with their
major axes from north to south. This gave more
room for the kitchen on the west: it also permitted a readjustment of the warming-house, and
left room at the east end for the insertion of a
wide and convenient day-stair to the dorter, with
a landing at the head, from which, as at Fountains,
access was given to a room, possibly the treasury or
muniment-room, above the warming-house. We have
no definite reason for the change of plan; but that it
was due to the uncontemplated growth of numbers in
Cistercian houses is at least probable. At Furness,
where the dorter was of remarkable length, the frater,
built in place of the old frater of the Savigniac
monastery, had to be lengthened during the thirteenth century, the only reason for which can have
been that, even on the new plan, it afforded insufficient room for all the brethren.

§ 64. The warming-house was a rectangular
building, which at Fountains is vaulted in four
compartments from a middle pillar. The fireplace

was usually in a side-wall or, as at Waverley, in the further wall from the cloister. Two huge fireplaces remain in the east wall at Fountains, one of which has been blocked. At Tintern the fireplace was a middle hearth, surrounded by open arches and connected by smaller arches with the end walls. The outer wall was generally pierced by a window and a doorway which led into a yard at the back. Here at Fountains, against the west wall of the dorter sub-vault, was the wood-house from which the fire was replenished. The west wall of the warming-house was part of the east wall of the frater, and two openings in it at Fountains may have been intended to give the frater some of the benefit of the fire. The arrangements of the frater, of which a perfect example, now used as a church, remains at Beaulieu, were similar, allowing for the difference in plan, to those of Benedictine and other houses, but were less elaborate. It was raised a step or two above the cloister, and on one or both sides of the entrance were the lavatory arches. The magnificent frater at Rievaulx had a sub-vault, entered from the foot of the stair to the pulpit; but this is a rare instance of a feature often found in Benedictine houses. At Fountains the frater was divided by a row of columns into two alleys, each with its separate wooden roof; but the undivided plan, as at Beaulieu, was general.

§ 65. The position of the kitchen was so planned as to communicate readily on one side with the monks' frater, which was served from it through a turn-table in the wall, and the frater of the lay brothers on the other, which was served at Fountains through a hatch in the west wall. It had a doorway from the cloister, which brought it into close connexion with the cellar and buttery in the western range; while at the back a door opened into a yard, where fuel could be kept. The fireplaces at Fountains and Kirkstall, where the kitchens were vaulted, were placed back to back in the middle of the room. Kitchens of the size of those at Durham or Glastonbury were unknown in Cistercian houses, where, even after the relaxation of the ordinary simple diet, meat was never cooked in the frater kitchen. The plan, which provided for the simultaneous supply of two fraters when necessary, was more compact and less secular in some of its features than the Benedictine plan; while the actual admission of the kitchen into the cloister buildings was made possible by the fact that the monks themselves did their own work, instead of using hired servants under the superintendence of the kitchener.

§ 66. The western range of a Cistercian cloister was sometimes separated from the west walk by an intervening passage or yard, as at Kirkstall, Pipewell and a few other houses, probably more in number

Fig. 12. Fountains abbey: *cellarium*, looking north.

than has been supposed. At the end of this yard
was the western processional doorway of the church,
the position of which depended on convenience for
the Sunday procession, which always passed outside
the west cloister, through the ground-floor of the
western range. If the church extended west of the
range, the doorway, as at Fountains, was in the
building itself, or, as at Jervaulx, where the building
did not directly join the church, in the bay west of it.
If the range was to the west of a short nave, as at
Hayles and Tintern, and there was no intermediate
yard, the doorway was cut obliquely through the
corner of the building which touched, or was near
the church. The whole of the first floor was given
up to the dorter of the lay brothers, to which was
attached a rere-dorter, the arrangements of which
are still remarkably perfect at Fountains. A night-
stair descended into the church, as at Fountains, or,
as at Jervaulx, just outside the western processional
doorway: in houses where there was an intervening
yard, the night-stair was placed against the east wall
of the range. The ground-floor was divided by a
passage, which was the outer parlour and main
entrance of the cloister and entered the west walk
close to the kitchen, into a long apartment on the
side furthest from the church, and into a series of
smaller rooms adjoining the church and cloister. The
large room was the frater of the lay brothers: the

rooms on the other side of the outer parlour were
the buttery and cellars, and could be entered by
doorways from the outer court and cloister-walk,
while there were doors in the partition-walls between
them. The building varied much in length. The
splendid example at Fountains is twenty-two bays
long, divided by columns into two alleys. The marks
of the original partitions and doorways shew that two
bays next the church were possibly the earlier outer
parlour. The cellar was in the four bays following.
Two bays were occupied by the buttery, two by the
main entrance-passage; while the remaining twelve
were the lay brothers' frater, two bays at the north
end of which were screened off and had an outer
doorway to the cellarer's checker. The western face
was covered by one of those wooden pentises which
were a very general feature in medieval buildings to
cover doorways from a court or yard and form a
sheltered means of access from one building to
another. The day-stair to the dorter was naturally
on this side of the building, and mounted against the
north wall of the cellarer's checker, the upper floor
of which was a lobby to the dorter. The arrangements at Furness were very similar, but there were
only fifteen bays, of which the cellar seems to have
occupied only two, the cloister-entry one, and the
lay-brothers' frater eight, the buttery and the two
bays next the church remaining as at Fountains.

The division into alleys, although it occasionally was employed, as at Furness and Waverley, was not general, and the building was frequently narrow in proportion to its length. When the cloister of Waverley was enlarged in the thirteenth century, the cellarer's building was taken down to make way for the west walk, but its southern part, containing the lay brothers' frater and dorter, was rebuilt and extended southward.

§ 67. In the later middle ages the Cistercian plan underwent some modification. The disappearance of lay brothers from the convents caused the disuse of a large part of the western range, which at Hayles was converted into the abbot's lodging. In some instances, as at Furness and Hayles, new processional doorways were made into the church from the west walk of the cloister, so that the course of the Sunday procession no longer differed from the Benedictine usage. At Waverley, on the other hand, after the destruction of the old cellarer's building, the procession still returned to the church outside the cloister, through a narrow passage between the cloister and an outer wall on the west. A further approximation to Benedictine use is seen in the fifteenth-century rebuilding of the frater at Cleeve upon a plan parallel to the church and adjacent cloister walk. Relaxation of discipline and the diminished number of monks allowed for more individual privacy: thus at Jervaulx some bays of the sub-dorter were cut off to form small rooms, each with its own fireplace. An important change was introduced in some houses owing to the removal of restrictions upon flesh-diet, which went so far that in the fifteenth century flesh was eaten on three days a week[1]. Hitherto a special flesh-frater or misericord (*misericordia*, i.e. indulgence) for monks undergoing bleeding had been provided in connexion with the infirmary buildings and kitchen. It now became convenient to place the misericord in closer communication with the cloister, and at Ford and Kirkstall this was done by dividing the frater into an upper and lower floor, the lower floor being probably used as the misericord. A new and smaller two-storied frater was built at Furness. In such cases meat was never cooked in the old kitchen, but a special meat-kitchen was provided; and the south end of the destroyed frater at Furness may have been kept for this purpose. At Jervaulx a new misericord was built at right angles to the east end of the frater, and a meat-kitchen was made about the same time on the other side of the sub-dorter.

§ 68. The chief peculiarities of the Cistercian

---

[1] In Benedictine houses the use of the misericord for monks in ordinary health was permitted at an earlier period. Abbot Colerne (1260–96) made regulations in 1292 for the daily use of the misericord at Malmesbury by a certain number of monks.

plan were without influence on the houses of other
orders, which adhered to Benedictine precedent in
such points as the position of the warming-house,
frater and kitchen. Thus the plan of the Augustinian
house of Haughmond, allowing for special exigencies
of site, is that of a Benedictine monastery, with the
exception that the building between the church and
chapter-house appears, as at St Agatha's and many
smaller monasteries, to have been a sacristy, while the
canons' parlour, as again at St Agatha's and at Repton,
was in the Cistercian position, south of the chapter-
house. At Alnwick the sacristy and parlour stood
side by side south of the church. Variations may be
found in such points as the connexion of the dorter
with the church: in the Carmelite friary of Hulne,
for example, the night-stair opened, not into the
church itself, but into a small court next it. But
the collation of plans, such as those of the Augustinian
St Frideswide's at Oxford and the Premonstratensian
St Radegund's at Bradsole, with those of other orders,
shews clearly that the arrangement of canons' and
friars' cloisters was modelled upon the convenient
Benedictine plan. The same conclusion applies to
nunneries, as may be gathered from the foregoing
pages. Little is known of the buildings of Cistercian
nunneries, but the nuns' cloister at Watton was upon
the Benedictine plan, with the exception that the
ground-floor of the western range was probably the

house of the lay sisters. The canons' cloister was very similar in plan; but its vaulted chapter-house, like others already mentioned, may shew the architectural influence of the Cistercian order. The two cloisters were connected by a long passage, in which was the turning-window (*fenestra versatilis*), where necessary communication was carried on between the two divisions of the monastery.

§ 69. The plan of the Carthusian cloister, however, owing to the solitary life prescribed by the rule, was unique. The monastery at Mount Grace consisted of two courts, the northern or cloister-court being surrounded on three sides by a series of separate cells, each with its own garden. On the south side were the chapter-house and the cells occupied by the sacrist and prior; while the frater occupied the south-west angle of the court. The church stood at the back of the chapter-house and part of the south range, next the outer court. The chapter-house was, in fact, a northern annexe to the church, parallel and almost exactly equal in dimensions to the presbytery. Some years after the foundation of the priory, owing to an increase in endowments and the number of monks, a second cloister was formed south of the church by enclosing a long rectangular space in the north-east part of the outer court: later still, the north-west angle of the same court was divided by partition walls into one or more courts covering the west front of the church and the west wall of the new cloister. The outer court, thus curtailed, contained as usual the storehouses of the convent, the building on the west side, through which the monastery was entered, being probably devoted to the use of guests.

CHAPTER V

THE INFIRMARY AND THE OUTER COURT

§ 70. Of the extra-claustral buildings of a monastery, the most important was the infirmary (*domus infirmaria, infirmitorium*). This was not merely used for the accommodation of the sick, but was the dwelling-place of those who were too infirm to take part in the regular routine of the cloister, known in most orders as *stagiarii* or *stationarii*, and of the *sempectae* who, in the Cistercian order, had been professed for fifty years. It was also generally used by the *minuti* or religious who were undergoing their periodical bleeding (*minutio*) for the sake of their health. Each of the Augustinian canons of Barnwell was allowed to be bled once every seven weeks, if he so desired: he might even be bled once a month, if his health demanded it, but in this latter case he was not allowed to take his furlough in the infirmary. The leave allowed at Barnwell lasted

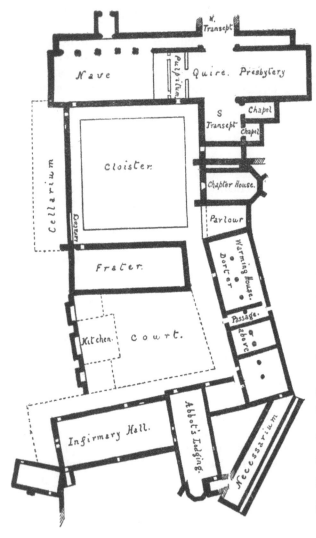

Fig. 13. Haughmond abbey: plan. N.B. The chapter-house was originally rectangular: the present ending was built after the suppression.

three days, and canons were permitted during such periods to talk to each other and take walks within a limited area[1]. Thus there were usually a few *minuti* on leave, whose absence made little difference to the number of those in quire; and in the larger houses it is clear that opportunities of bleeding took place once a week. In the Cistercian and Carthusian orders the rules were stricter: the monks were bled in batches appointed by the prior at fixed seasons in the year—four seasons in Cistercian, five in Carthusian monasteries. According to the statutes, Cistercian *minuti* were obliged to take their meals in the frater, but this rule appears to have been gradually relaxed, and monks probably went into the infirmary, as in other orders, and were allowed a flesh-diet[2]. In Cluniac houses the actual operation of bleeding took place in the common house. Several Benedictine houses—e.g. Bardney and Croyland— sent their *minuti* to small houses or granges at a little distance from the monastery, under the supervision of a prior.

---

[1] Jocelyn of Brakelond says that in bleeding-time 'monks are wont to open to one another the secrets of the heart and to take counsel together,' and describes how at such a time, in the vacancy before his election as abbot of Bury, Samson the sub-sacrist sat in silence, smiling at the gossip of the brethren.

[2] Abbot Paul (1077–98) ordained that the *minuti* at St Albans, instead of feeding on meat pasties, should have a dish of salt-fish and slices of cake, known as 'karpie.'

§ 71. The buildings of the infirmary, known colloquially as the 'farmery,' consisted of a hall, chapel and kitchen, close to which was usually a hall in which the convent might eat flesh-meat on certain days. This hall was commonly called the misericord: it was known at Canterbury as the *deportum* and at Peterborough as the 'seyny.' As already stated, access to these buildings, which formed a self-contained group, was obtained by a passage through the east range of the cloister or at the further end of the east walk. Their position, however, was dictated by convenience, and they followed no very consistent plan. Thus, at Durham and Worcester, where the dorter was west of the cloister, the infirmary was also on the west side, between the cloister and the river. At Canterbury the infirmary was on the east side of a smaller eastern cloister, of which the west side was occupied by the great dorter and its sub-vault, the north side by the second or obedientiaries' dorter, and the south side by the laver-house and the night-passage to the church on the upper floor of the cloister. The infirmary at Gloucester was entered from the north-east side of a small cloister north of the great cloister. At Peterborough it was a detached building to the north-east of the cloister. In Cistercian abbeys it was generally connected with the east walk of the cloister by a long covered gallery or passage, which usually threw off a branch, nearly at right angles, to the eastern part of the church. The twelfth-century infirmary at Rievaulx is in this position, and its plan, with the major axis north and south and a chapel opening from it on the eastern side, was followed in the later infirmary at Fountains. But at Jervaulx the earlier infirmary appears to have been beneath the rere-dorter, and its successor formed an eastern continuation of the same building. Similarly, at Netley there is a hall with a great fireplace beneath the rere-dorter. At Furness, where the eastern part of the site is much contracted, the old infirmary, to the south-east, was converted into a lodging for the abbot: the new infirmary, with its chapel, was built south of the cloister in the fourteenth century. In Cistercian houses a special infirmary was also needed for the lay brothers: the remains of this at Fountains are on the west side of the western cloister-range, with which they are connected by the lay brothers' rere-dorter.

§ 72. The infirmary hall in its simplest form was an aisleless oblong, on either side of which was a row of beds. From the east side or end opened the infirmary chapel. The hall, however, was sometimes too wide to be roofed in one span without support, and consequently aisled halls became very usual, divided either by regular arcades with a clerestory above or by upright posts of wood. The beds were

Fig. 14. Peterborough: infirmary, looking west.

placed within the aisles, the nave forming a central
gangway. This was a common plan in medieval
hospitals, many of which were quasi-conventual
establishments following the rule of St Augustine:
St Mary's hospital at Chichester, a long hall running
east and west, with a wooden roof of one span
supported on each side of the nave by upright posts
which are bound together by longitudinal trusses,
and with an aisleless chapel screened off at the east
end, is a famous surviving example of its use. At
Ely and Canterbury the Norman infirmaries were
divided by stone arcades and clerestoried; while at
Gloucester and Peterborough there are substantial
remains of aisled infirmaries of the thirteenth century.
Most of the south aisle at Peterborough is now included in one of the canons' houses, while the chapel
at the east end of the infirmary forms the dining-
room of another. In the infirmary hall at Fountains,
which ran north and south, with the chapel and
kitchen on its eastern side, the arcades were returned
across the ends, and there were large fireplaces in the
end walls. A fireplace was a necessity, and, where
no original fireplaces can be traced in the side or
end walls, there was presumably a middle hearth,
the smoke from which escaped through a louvre in
the roof. As a rule the beds were arranged at right
angles to the side walls. At Furness, however, where
there were no arcades and the hall was lighted by

windows in the upper part of the walls, the north and south walls contained a number of arched recesses near the floor, each lighted by a small window and wide enough to contain a bed with its side against the wall. Similar recesses have been noted in a portion of the east aisle of the infirmary of the lay brothers at Fountains, against the end wall of the lay brothers' rere-dorter. In later days it became the general custom to divide the aisles into separate rooms, often with their own fireplaces. This was usual by the beginning of the fifteenth century: it is known to have been done at Meaux before 1396, and there is much evidence for it in the Lincoln episcopal registers of the next fifty years. At Canterbury the south aisle was walled up before 1400 and divided into rooms as a lodging for the sub-prior. In Cistercian infirmaries, as at Fountains, Kirkstall, Tintern and Waverley, there are abundant traces of this practice. A peculiar arrangement was adopted in the fourteenth-century infirmary at Westminster, where the hall was removed and a number of separate rooms were arranged round a cloister, the aisled chapel of the hall being retained on the east side. At Jervaulx, where the infirmary hall was not large, part of the sub-vault of the dorter was partitioned off into separate rooms, probably as an annexe to the infirmary.

§ 73. A special kitchen, where more delicate

food (*cibi subtiliores*) could be cooked for the infirm, was a necessary adjunct to an infirmary, and is usually found divided from it by a narrow yard, crossed by a covered passage, as at Fountains. The infirmary kitchen at Furness was octagonal, but the normal plan was rectangular. The Furness kitchen served the old infirmary: when this was converted into the abbot's lodging and a new infirmary built, it probably served both; but in the fifteenth century a kitchen was made in the abbot's lodging, the octagonal kitchen seems to have been taken down, and the infirmary was probably served from a meat-kitchen which, as has been explained in the previous chapter, also served the new frater and misericord. The misericord or flesh-frater had no fixed position in the plan of the infirmary buildings. At Fountains, it was an aisleless hall, lying between the infirmary hall and the abbot's lodging, and must have been served through the infirmary hall from the kitchen.

§ 74.   Heads of religious houses were provided, as time went on, with separate lodgings (*camerae*, i.e. chambers), which, as has been seen, frequently occupied or were partly upon the upper floor of the western cloister-range. In Cistercian abbeys, where the western range had its own use, the abbot's *camera* was very generally built, as is recorded of Croxden and Meaux, on the east side of the dorter, between the eastern cloister-range and the infirmary. As the

first floor of the lodging generally communicated
with the monks' rere-dorter, the spirit, if not the
letter, of the custom which required Cistercian
abbots to sleep in the dorter was still observed.
The construction of these separate lodgings in
Cistercian monasteries seems to have become general
towards the beginning of the fourteenth century;
but at Kirkstall there is a three-storied house of the
middle of the thirteenth century, standing between the
rere-dorter and an eastern building of somewhat
earlier date in which were additional rooms and
the abbot's chapel. At Fountains the abbot's lodging
was made by remodelling an older block of buildings
between the dorter and the infirmary. Additions
were made to this in later times: the living rooms
were upon the first floor and must have included the
abbot's great chamber or solar and his bedroom and
chapel or oratory. It has been suggested that he
used the misericord, to which there was a passage
from the ground-floor of his lodging, as his hall for
the entertainment of guests; and monastic visitations
shew that in houses of other orders the abbot's hall
was sometimes used as the misericord. The upper
floor of the long passage which led from the cloister
to the infirmary at Fountains was apparently the
gallery of the abbot's lodging, and another gallery
over the passage which branched off to the church
led to a pew overlooking the nine altars, which allowed

the abbot and his guests to hear mass without leaving
his lodging. The connexion with the dorter, which
was to some extent preserved at Fountains, was
entirely severed at Furness, where the old infirmary
hall was converted into the abbot's hall, and a new
block, containing his great chamber, chapel and bedroom was built on the narrow space between the hall
and the low cliff on the east. It has been noted before
that the western range at Hayles was turned into an
abbot's lodging. The same change took place at
Ford, where, not long before the suppression, abbot
Chard built the magnificent abbot's hall, which,
extending westwards from the site of the lay-
brothers' frater, forms part of the existing dwelling-
house. Evidence of additional *camerae* is often
found in the neighbourhood of the abbot's lodging
and infirmary of Cistercian houses, as at Kirkstall,
Furness and Waverley. These may have been applied
to the use of the visiting abbot; but it is clear that
in houses of other orders, as in the Cluniac priory of
Daventry, such lodgings were appropriated to abbots
or priors who had resigned their office, and this may
account for the existence of more than one such
camera at Furness[1].

§ 75. The normal position of the abbot's lodging

---

[1] At St Albans there was a large *camera* for infirm abbots close to
the infirmary. This, known as the *pictorium* or painted chamber,
was destroyed by the insurgent tenants in 1381.

in monasteries of other orders was, however, west of the cloister. Exceptional positions are found, for example at Haughmond, where the thirteenth-century abbot's lodging was a building south of the cloister, nearly parallel with the dorter and its sub-vault. The abbot seems to have used the ground floor, while the upper floor was used as part of the infirmary, the great hall of which, parallel with the frater, adjoined it on the west. In canons' houses, however, the abbot or prior might entertain his guests in the frater, and there was consequently no need for the large hall which was a feature of his lodging in the great Benedictine houses. In these, and especially in monasteries where pilgrimages were frequent, considerable provision had to be made for housing guests. In such houses as Canterbury, Durham and Worcester, where the prior was the actual head, under the archbishop or bishop, of the cathedral priory, he had his own lodging with its hall and guest-chambers. At Durham and Worcester these were to the south-east of the cloister, near the great gatehouse of the monastery: at Canterbury the prior's lodging was at the north-east angle of the infirmary cloister, where it is shewn in the famous Norman plan of the monastery. The same plan shews another building further east, called the *nova camera prioris*, divided from the older lodging by the kitchen and *necessarium* of the infirmary. This

was the prior's guest-house. Both lodgings underwent much enlargement, and a third lodging or
guest-house, which is now the deanery, was built
by prior Goldstone (1495–1517) on a site north of the
infirmary and north-east of the old lodging. The
ruins of the prior's guest-house at Worcester still
remain: it was destroyed as recently as 1860. The
older abbot's lodging at Gloucester, west of the
cloister, was in course of time devoted to the prior,
while the abbot built himself a new house north of
the monastery. As at Peterborough, the abbot's
lodging became in 1541 the bishop's palace, while
the prior's lodging was appropriated to the dean. In
monasteries where cathedral chapters were founded
by Henry VIII, the prior's lodging, as at Durham,
was usually occupied by the dean. It was the
deanery at Worcester until some seventy years ago,
when the dean removed to the old bishop's palace on
the north-west side of the cathedral. Part of it is
used as the deanery at Ely: the prior's chapel, built
in 1325–6 by prior John of Crauden, adjoins a
portion of the lodging now converted into a canon's
house.

§ 76. The hospitality of the abbot or prior, however, was accorded only to distinguished guests. For
the more ordinary type of guest a special hostry or
guest-house (*hospitium*) was built in the outer court.
In the ninth-century plan of St Gall, there are two

hostries, one on each side of the main entrance, one
of which was the general guest-house, while the other
was the lodging for the poor.   At Canterbury this
double division of guest-houses existed.   On the west
side of the outer court, immediately to the left of
the main gatehouse, was the hall known as the north
hall, a long building with a sub-vault, entered by a
covered stair which is one of the most celebrated
examples of Anglo-Norman architecture.   This, in
close connexion with the almonry, is generally recognised to have been the casual ward, to borrow a
modern term, of the monastery.   From the other side
of the gatehouse, a pentise along the west wall of the
court formed a covered way towards the north-west
angle of the cloister, where a small gatehouse gave
admission to a court between the kitchen on the east
and the cellarer's guest-hall on the west.   About the
beginning of the fifteenth century, the accommodation
for guests under charge of the cellarer was enlarged
by the building of a range of guest-chambers on the
north side of the kitchen[1].   In the *Rites of Durham*
there is no mention of a special guest-house in connexion with the almonry ; but there is a description

---

[1] Abbot Brokehampton (1282–1316) built two guest-chambers
at Evesham upon vaulted undercrofts on the west side of the *curia*.
In 1878 parliament sat in the guest-house and other buildings at
Gloucester : the account shews how the cloister life was disorganised
by the crowd of visitors.

of the guest-house on the east side of the *curia*, with
its aisled hall and central fireplace, and its separate
chambers or lodgings. It was served from the prior's
kitchen and was conveniently situated with regard to
the cellarer's checker and the cellar. The guests,
however, were as a rule under charge, not of the
cellarer, but of a special guest-master or hosteller
(*hostilarius*), who was known at Durham as the
terrer (*terrarius*), a name implying other duties in
connexion with the lands of the monastery. The
office of the hosteller is minutely described in the
customs of the Augustinian priory of Barnwell: he
had complete supervision of the guest-house and its
furniture, and was in close communication with the
cellarer and kitchener, from whom he obtained
supplies for his guests. In Cistercian abbeys the usual
division between classes of guests appears to have
been observed: thus at Fountains and Kirkstall
there are remains of two guest-houses in the outer
court. A special infirmary for lay-folk was a feature
of Cistercian monasteries, and at Fountains there
seems also to have been an infirmary for the poor.
A Benedictine infirmary for lay-folk existed at
Durham, where it stood outside the monastery
gates.

§ 77. In addition to the guest-houses, the outer
court generally contained the brew-house, the bake-
house and granary of the monastery. In Cistercian

houses, where the statutes required that all the offices should be within the precinct, there was generally another court outside the main gatehouse. In the great monastery of Clairvaux this additional court was of large extent and included workshops and smithies with numerous other offices. It may be seen on a smaller scale at Beaulieu, where the mill of the monastery adjoins the outer gatehouse, and at Furness. There was frequently, near the outer gateway and, as at Furness and Fountains, just within it, a chapel (*capella extra portas*), provided for the use of persons not allowed within the great gateway. Such chapels, at Merevale in Warwickshire and Tiltey in Essex, were enlarged in the later middle ages to serve as parish churches. At Kirkstead in Lincolnshire the chapel is perfect, though now disused, and chapels at Coggeshall and Rievaulx have been repaired and are used for service. At Beaulieu and Whalley there was a chapel upon the first floor of the main gatehouse, and one was begun at Meaux to supersede an older *capella extra portas*[1]. Such chapels are to be distinguished from the parish churches which are often found, as at Bury St Edmunds or Coventry and in the small example at Barnwell priory, close to the precinct of a religious house.

§ 78.   Monasteries of other orders were generally

---

[1] This was due to the removal of a chantry of six monks and a secular priest from Ottringham to the monastery.

content with a single outer court, although there is evidence, for example at Gloucester, of some of the offices being arranged round a smaller court entered from the *curia*[1]. The great gatehouse of the *curia*, of which many fine examples remain, was the main entrance to the monastery, and was usually a building with one or more upper floors and a vaulted passage or gate-hall on the ground-floor. In the earlier examples, as at Peterborough, the gateway was a single wide arch, as is also the case in the early fourteenth-century gatehouse at Kirkham. This gave entrance to carriages and foot-passengers alike. Later gate-houses were built on a larger scale, and the gate-hall was entered by a wide portal with a low doorway or postern at the side for pedestrians, as at Bridlington, Christchurch gate, Canterbury, Torre, and St Albans. On one side of the gate-hall was the porter's lodge. Occasionally, as at Peterborough, the chamber on the upper floor was used as a chapel. The finest of all existing English examples is the gatehouse at Thornton, remarkable for the barbican which gives it as important a place in military as in monastic architecture; but the Christchurch and St Augustine's

---

[1] In Benedictine monasteries there were usually several offices outside the precinct—e.g., at Tewkesbury the mill and the guests' stable, burned in 1257, were *extra portam abbatiae*. The building of permanent offices in the *curia* at Bury by abbot Samson is described by Jocelyn of Brakelond.

gatehouses at Canterbury, and the two gatehouses at Bury St Edmunds are hardly second to it in interest and beauty.   The southern and earlier

Fig. 15.   Kirkham priory: gatehouse.

gatehouse at Bury was the *porta coemeterii* directly opposite the west front of the church, and is a square

Norman tower, not unlike the great tower of a
Norman castle: the northern gatehouse, built in the
fourteenth century, was the entrance to the outer
court of the monastery. Large monasteries were
frequently provided with more than one outer gatehouse: thus the Christchurch gateway at Canterbury
was the entrance to the cathedral and the part of the
churchyard set apart for lay burials, while the main
gatehouse was in the western wall of the outer court.
Special entrances to the lay-folks' cemetery are also
found at Gloucester and Rochester; while at Norwich,
as at Bury, one of the two western gateways leads
directly to the cathedral, while the other was the
main entrance to the precinct.

§ 79. Close to the gatehouse of the *curia*, and,
as at Canterbury, immediately outside it, was the
almonry (*domus elemosinaria*), where the daily dole
of broken meat from the tables of the monastery was
given to the poor by the almoner (*elemosinarius*).
The almoner at Durham had control of the infirmary
without the gate, where four old women were
maintained. Such monastic almshouses, which had
parallels in the bede-houses attached to some
secular colleges in the later middle ages, were not
uncommon: it is clear, from a passage in the Ripon
chapter act-book, that the chamber over the outer
gateway at Fountains was used for the same purpose. In the upper part of the almonry at Durham

were lodged the 'children of the almery,' who were educated at the expense of the monastery and were taught daily in the outer infirmary. Elsewhere, as at Barnwell and Thornton, these children were known as the clerks of the almonry, and their position was similar to that of the *clerici secundae formae*, who in secular colleges were under the direction of the chancellor. They were educated with the intention of entering holy orders. Some of them, no doubt, became novices in the monastery, but ordination lists shew that many of them became secular clergy, who obtained their titles to orders from the religious houses in which they had received their education. In 1431 a papal dispensation was granted to the abbot and convent of St Augustine's, Canterbury, to build a grammar school outside their gates for the poor boys of their almonry and to appoint a special master or rector, and it is evident that, although there was some doubt as to the canonical propriety of the application of alms in this direction, the education of poor children was a common part of the activity of monasteries[1].

---

[1] The almonry at St Albans, built by abbot Wallingford (1326–35), included a hall, chapel, chambers, kitchen, cellar and other buildings necessary for the scholars and their master.

CHAPTER VI

DISCIPLINE AND THE DAILY LIFE

§ 80.   The chief object of this book has been to explain the position and use of the various buildings of a monastery, and in its course reference has been made to several leading features of the life which was led within them.   The sketch may be completed by some brief notes on the arrangements for monastic discipline and the ordinary life of the house.   The abbot was the head and father of the house, who presided in chapter and was responsible for the due correction of erring brethren and the treatment of the complaints which monks and canons were encouraged to make publicly in the daily chapter-meeting.   His duties, however, were largely delegated to the prior, who was the officer charged with the maintenance of order in the cloister[1].   Where the prior was head of the house, the sub-prior took this secondary position.   In monasteries where the number of brethren was large, as at Lewes or Peterborough, the prior was helped in the cloister by other monks, who were known as the sub-prior and the third and

[1] The prior was usually nominated by the abbot, or the names of several nominees were submitted to the convent for election. Jocelyn of Brakelond gives a detailed account of the election of a prior at Bury.

fourth prior.   An old name for the junior priors was
circae or *circatores*: their duty was to make periodical
rounds of inspection in the cloister and dorter.   But,
in addition to these disciplinary officers, there were
other officials, each of whom administered a special
department of the convent.   Their offices, held by
commission from the abbot, were called obediences
(*obedientiae*), and they themselves were known
collectively as obedientiaries (*obedientiarii*).   In the
great monasteries the abbot had his own household
officers, chosen from the monks: at Peterborough in
1440 he had his own seneschal, receiver or bailiff,
cellarer, chamberlain, and chaplain[1].   Of the obedientiaries usually found in connexion with the convent,
two, the precentor and sacrist, were in charge of the
church.   The precentor was responsible for the singing,
the direction of processions and the repair and proper
notation of the quire-books: he also, as at Barnwell,
filled the office of librarian (*armarius*).   The sacrist
had control of the clock, bells, lights and ornaments
of the church.   They were sometimes assisted in
their offices by a succentor or sub-chanter and

---

[1] The abbot's household at Gloucester, as regulated by archbishop
Winchelsey in 1301, included five lay esquires and several lay
servants, each with a definite office.   Of the esquires one was
seneschal of the guest-hall, another marshal, who was charged with
regulating accounts, a third cook: the other two were appointed to
serve the abbot's table and bed-chamber.

sub-sacrist. The sacrist at Peterborough was excused from attendance in quire save on certain festivals. The same excuse applied for more obvious reasons to the cellarer and almoner, and to the monks who filled the offices of treasurer and master of the works, the second of whom controlled the repairs of the church and monastery. The cellarer and almoner were invariably found in all monasteries. The cellarer was the chief means of communication between the house and the world outside: he marketed and went to fairs, and bought the necessary provisions and furniture. The duties of the almoner have already been noticed: he and the cellarer were frequently assisted by a sub-almoner and sub-cellarer. The cellarer, whose checker was usually in the neighbourhood of the *cellarium* and kitchen, was in close touch with the fraterer (*refectorarius*) and kitchener (*coquinarius*), whose chief duties were to arrange the meals in the frater and to regulate the activities of the cook and his assistants[1]. He also was, as we have seen, responsible in some degree for the hospitality of the house, which was administered directly by the hosteller (*hostilarius*). Equally necessary to the conduct of the monastery were the infirmarer (*infirmarius*), who looked after the brethren in the infirmary and sometimes, as at Peterborough, had

[1] Thus the cellarer of Evesham supplied the frater daily with 72 loaves.

his separate lodging in its neighbourhood, and the chamberlain (*camerarius*), who attended to the clothes of the brethren and their bedding in the dorter. The receiver (*receptor*), treasurer (*thesaurarius*) or bursar (*bursarius*) collected rents in money: the garnerer or granger (*granatarius*) collected the tithe in corn which belonged to the monastery, and supplied the cellarer with his stores of bread and beer. These offices of course varied in different houses, and in the later middle ages some are found in combination; but, as the needs of all orders were to some extent the same, the differences are trifling[1]. Each was bound to render an account of his administration yearly or quarterly, and, where such accounts survive, the information which they give is from the social and economical point of view of the highest value.

§ 81. The time-table of a monastic day in church and cloister must be reckoned with attention to the fact that the day, between sunrise and sunset, was divided, irrespective of the season, into twelve equal parts. The hours in winter were thus some twenty

[1] The officers and obedientiaries at Evesham in the thirteenth century were the prior, sub-prior, third prior and other *custodes ordinis*, the precentor, dean of the Christianity of the vale of Evesham, sacrist, chamberlain, kitchener, two cellarers, infirmarer, almoner, warden of the vineyard and garden, master of the fabric, guest-master and pittancer. The last official distributed the money allowances of the brethren.

minutes shorter than in summer, and, with this in
view, a different arrangement was adopted during the
winter months, which began on Holy Cross day
(14 September) and lasted till Easter. Artificial light
was impossible in the cloister after sunset, and consequently in winter the brethren went to bed earlier.
Their night was divided into two equal portions,
between which came the night-office of matins followed
by lauds. The rule of St Benedict contemplated an
undivided night, with matins as the first day-office,
said before daybreak; but the general practice followed
in all orders was to rise in the middle of the night
for matins and to return to the dorter afterwards.
At Durham the monks rose by the light of cressets—
bowls filled with oil and floating wicks, and set in
hollows in square stone stands at either end of the
dorter. In most monasteries the brethren entered
and left the church in procession before and after
matins by the night-stair, and the time between
dressing and the signal to go to church was occupied
in private prayer. After preparatory psalms, the
service began with the invitatory, which included the
psalm *Venite exultemus*. It was divided into nocturns,
each consisting of a group of psalms followed by three
lessons : on ordinary days matins consisted of a single
nocturn, but on most feast-days there were three.
Lauds followed: this service derived its name from
the three final psalms of the psalter, known from

their opening words, *Laudate Dominum*, as the *laudes*. The whole night-office was of considerable length—equal, in fact, to that of the day-hours taken together—and was further increased by the addition of the office of our Lady and on certain days of *Placebo*, or matins of the dead. When it was over, the brethren returned to bed and rose, at daybreak in winter, at sunrise in summer, for prime, when the sub-prior unlocked the day-stair and the church was entered by the ordinary doorway from the cloister.

§ 82. The day-hours were said every three hours, as their names imply—prime at the first, terce at the third, sext at the sixth, none at the ninth. In summer prime was followed in Benedictine and Cistercian houses by chapter. This began with the versicle *Pretiosa* ('Right dear in the sight of the Lord is the death of His saints') which preceded the martyrology or account of the saints commemorated on the day: this was followed by the necrology, or list of the dead to be remembered, and by a chapter of the rule with a sermon or commentary. The work of each monk was allotted for the day, and the meeting closed with *clamationes* or individual complaints, public confessions and corrections by the head of the house. The interval between chapter and terce was occupied by the monks in work in the cloister or in their various offices. Terce was followed by the chapter mass, during which at Durham half the monks in

priest's orders said their private masses. The other
half said their masses during high mass, which was
sung about an hour after the chapter mass and
immediately before sext. During this time, no food
was taken. Bread soaked in wine (*mixtum*) was
allowed to those whose strength was hardly equal to
the long morning. In the Premonstratensian order,
where, as in Augustinian houses, the chapter mass
seems to have been sung immediately after prime,
and chapter was followed after an interval by terce,
the *mixtum* was distributed after terce to the infirm
and the novices. All spare intervals were filled by
work, and silence was rigorously maintained, all
necessary conversation taking place in the parlour.

§ 83. The first meal (*prandium*) took place at
mid-day in the frater, soon after sext. During the
meal the reader for the week, who had taken his
repast before the rest, occupied the pulpit and read
from the Bible or some pious book. Grace after meat
ended with the *Miserere*, which was sung in procession through the cloister, the concluding collect
and suffrages being said in church. The brethren
then retired to rest in the dorter, until none. Work
of various kinds filled up the time between none and
vespers, a service which corresponded in its general
structure to lauds. After vespers and the usual grace
came supper (*caena*). During the interval between
supper and compline (*completorium*), the last office,

the convent met in the chapter-house for collation, at
which the *Collationes* of Cassian or a chapter from
some other monastic author were read. Compline
ended the day, although, in times of lax discipline,
there arose a custom of sitting up late in the warming-
house which called for correction from episcopal
visitors. The strict rule, however, required that the
brethren should repair directly after compline to the
dorter, and that all doors in the church and cloister
should be locked until prime. At Durham the sub-
prior went the round of the dorter towards the middle
of the night to see that all was in good order. The
rule required constant vigilance on the part of the
officers, especially with regard to the maintenance of
silence and the prevention of the accumulation of
private property by the brethren.

§ 84. In winter the morning or chapter mass was
sung between prime and terce, and terce was succeeded
by chapter. High mass and sext followed. Between
sext and none the convent was at work. After none
came the mid-day meal, and the rest of the day was
spent as usual until compline, with the omission of
the post-prandial rest, which in a season of long nights
was not needed. In orders in which manual labour
played a large part—the Cistercian and Premonstratensian, for example—special portions of the day
were set aside for such work. The Cistercians worked
in the morning between chapter and terce, and in the

afternoon between none and vespers. In winter they usually worked from chapter after terce till none, apparently saying sext privately: in Lent they also said none at their work, and did not have their meal until after vespers. Their periods for reading and contemplation were an interval between matins and lauds in all seasons, the time between the morning mass and sext in summer (for in this order there seems to have originally been no high mass before sext), and part of the interval between vespers and compline. Premonstratensian canons worked in summer from chapter to terce, and in hay-time and harvest spent the greater part of the day in the fields, saying their hours privately, and dining and sleeping in the granges, if necessary. In winter work was done after terce. The Premonstratensian hours for reading were between sext and the mid-day meal in summer or none in winter, and again after none or the mid-day meal till vespers. In the summer the canons were allowed their daily bevers or draught of wine before vespers in the frater. The conduct of the daily life in the various orders applies equally to houses of female religious, where the officers corresponded to those in male convents, the night and day-hours were said and chapters were held on the same model, and the only important difference was that chaplains had to be imported to say mass and hear private confessions, the hour for which in all orders was usually after chapter.

§ 85. It is probable that the observances of all
orders in the two centuries before the suppression
tended to become very similar. Records of visitations
in the fifteenth century shew that there had grown to
be scarcely any difference between the ordinary
customs of Benedictine monks and Augustinian
canons: injunctions delivered to a house of one order
were repeated in almost the same terms to a house of
another. The Carthusian order stood apart from the
rest, however, by virtue of its ascetic rule—a rule
stricter and more frugal even than that followed by
the early Cistercians. Each monk lived his own life
in his cell, going to church for the night-office, the
early masses and vespers, and to the frater for the
mid-day meal and supper on Sundays and certain
feast-days, but otherwise saying his offices alone and
served with his two meals a day through a hatch
in the wall of his cell. On Sundays and chapter
festivals all the hours, except compline, were said in
church, and two chapters were held, one after prime
and the second after none. In this life of lonely
austerity, given up to contemplation and precluded
even from the field-work and farming which were
part of the activity of the strictest orders, later
medieval sentiment found much to admire ; and the
popularity of the Carthusians in the fourteenth and
fifteenth centuries was probably a recognition of their
maintenance of the primitive simplicity from which
the older and greater houses had declined.

BIBLIOGRAPHY

The literature of the whole subject is vast, and allusion can be made here only to works bearing directly on English monastic history and buildings. The names of several works not mentioned here will be found in C. Gross' invaluable bibliography of *The Sources and Literature of English History from the earliest times to about 1485*, 2nd ed., 1915.

A. EARLY MONASTIC HISTORY. See *Cambridge Medieval History*, vol. I, pp. 521–42 (by Dom E. C. Butler, abbot of Downside). A full bibliography will be found on pp. 683–7 of the same volume.

B. RELIGIOUS ORDERS. (1) Benedictine monks. The rule of St Benedict has been edited by Dom E. C. Butler, Freiburg-im-Breisgau, 1911. There is a translation by cardinal Gasquet in the 'King's Classics' series. See also Dom E. C. Butler's *Benedictine Monachism*, 1919, and the English translation (1921) of Dom Paul Delatte's *Commentary on the Rule of St Benedict*.

(2) Carthusian monks. See H. V. le Bas in *Yorks. Archaeol. Journal*, XVIII, 241–52.

(3) Cistercian monks. See *Cistercian Statutes*, ed. J. T. Fowler, 1890 (reprinted from *Yorks. Archaeol. Journal*, with preface containing references to original sources). See also J. T. Micklethwaite, *The Cistercian Order* (*Yorks. Archaeol. Journal*, XV, 245–68, reprinted as separate pamphlet). The most important collections of Cistercian statutes are *Nomasticon Cisterciense*, 1664, new ed., Solesmes, 1892; and P. Guignard's *Les Monuments Primitifs de la règle Cistercienne*, Dijon, 1878.

(4) Augustinian canons. The letter of St Augustine on which the rule was founded is no. ccxi in his *Epistolae*, printed with his other works in Migne, *Patrologiae Latinae Cursus*. The rule is printed by J. W. Clark, *Observances in Use at the Augustinian Priory of S. Giles and S. Andrew at Barnwell, Cambridgeshire*, Cambridge, 1897, pp. 2–23: see also the introduction to the same volume, pp. xxxi–civ, for a description of the customs of the order.

(5) Gilbertine canons. See Rose Graham, *St Gilbert of Sempringham and the Gilbertines*, 1902.

(6) Premonstratensian canons. See F. A. Gasquet, *Collectanea Anglo-Premonstratensia*, 3 vols., 1906 (Camden Soc., 3rd ser.). Some of the statutes are printed by J. W. Clark, *op. cit.* pp. 101–4.

(7) Nuns. See Lina Eckenstein, *Women and Monasticism*, Cambridge, 1896, and Eileen Power, *Medieval English Nunneries*, Cambridge, 1922.

(8) Friars. See *Monumenta Franciscana*, 2 vols., 1858, 1882 (Rolls ser.), ed. J. S. Brewer and R. Howlett; and the monograph by Dom Bede Jarrett on *The English Dominicans*, 1921.

A number of general documents of great importance are prefixed to the accounts of individual houses of the several orders in Dugdale's *Monasticon Anglicanum*, 8 vols., 1817–30, ed. Caley, Ellis and Bandinel —e.g. the Carthusian *Tractatus statutorum...pro noviciis*, and the *Vita* and *Institutiones Sancti Gileberti* prefixed to the accounts of houses of the order of Sempringham.

C. ENGLISH MONASTERIES: HISTORY. Dugdale, *Monasticon, ut sup.*, contains the text of a great number of documents, taken from various sources, relating to the large majority of English religious houses, together with a carefully annotated account of each house and a list of its heads. These accounts and lists have been supplemented and to some extent superseded by the articles upon the several religious houses which are contained in the published volumes of the *Victoria History of the Counties of England*, now in progress. The documents are in great part selected from the ms. chartularies of the various monasteries, of which many have been preserved in public and private collections.

Some chartularies have been printed in full—e.g. the Surtees Society has published those of Newminster, Rievaulx and Whitby abbeys, and of Brinkburn, Guisbrough and St Bees priories; the chartulary of Eynsham Abbey has been published by the Oxford Historical Society; those of Fountains and Bridlington have been privately printed by the late W. T. Lancaster; and chartularies of Gloucester, Hyde and Ramsey abbeys, and the register of Malmesbury abbey have appeared in the Rolls series. *Memorials of Fountains Abbey*, 2 vols., ed. J. R. Walbran, and *The Priory of Hexham*, 2 vols., ed. J. Raine (Surtees Soc.), contain collections of charters in addition to other historical matter.

A bibliograpy of some of the most important sources for the history of the monastic life is prefixed to cardinal Gasquet's *English Monastic Life*, 1904, a valuable account of the constitution and customs of religious houses, followed by an appendix containing the most complete list which has yet appeared of English monastic foundations. An annotated list (*The English Student's Monasticon*) forms vol. II of Mackenzie E. C. Walcott's *English Minsters*, 1879.

A large number of monastic chronicles have been printed in the Rolls series. The period before the Norman conquest is represented by the *Chronicon Monasterii de Abingdon*, Thomas of Elmham's *Historia Monasterii S. Augustini Cantuariensis*, the *Liber Monasterii de Hyda*, the *Chronicle of the Abbey of Ramsey*, and the *Vita S. Oswaldi* (in *Historians of the Church of York*, vol. I). Later history is contained in the *Annales Monastici*, 5 vols. (Annals of Bermondsey, Burton, Margam, Oseney, Tewkesbury and Waverley abbeys, and of Dunstable, Winchester and Worcester priories), the *Chronicon Abbatiae de Evesham*, *Historia et Cartularium Monasterii S. Petri Gloucestriae*, 3 vols., *Chronicon Monasterii de Melsa* (Meaux), 3 vols., Walsingham's *Gesta Abbatum Monasterii S. Albani*, 3 vols., *Registra quorundam abbatum S. Albani* (15 cent.), 2 vols., and *Memorials of St Edmund's Abbey*, 3 vols. Jocelyn of Brakelond's and other chronicles were printed by the Camden Society among their publications: there is a translation of Jocelyn in the 'King's Classics.'

For custom-books, monastic account-books, etc., reference may be made to cardinal Gasquet's bibliography, ut. sup., where also there are notes of printed editions of monastic visitations and episcopal registers. The registers of archbisbishops Giffard, Wickwane and Romeyn of York (ed. W. Brown for the Surtees Soc.) contain many valuable documents relating to visitations of monasteries. The present writer is engaged upon an edition of similar documents from the Lincoln Record Soc., of which vols. I and II (1420–49) have been published.

Other books of recent times are of the highest importance to students of monastic history, viz. (1) J. W. Clark's *Observances of Barnwell*, already mentioned; (2) *Inventories of Christ Church, Canterbury*, ed. Sir W. H. St John Hope and J. Wickham Legg, 1902; (3) *The Rites of Durham*, ed. J. T. Fowler, 1903 (Surt. Soc.), the notes to which are a mine of information as to monastic customs, ritual, etc.; (4) *Customary of the Benedictine Monasteries of St Augustine's, Canterbury and St Peter's Westminster*, ed. Maunde Thompson, 1902–4 (Henry Bradshaw Soc.); (5) *Chapters of the Augustinian Canons*, ed. H. E. Salter, 1922 (Cant. and York Soc.).

D. ENGLISH MONASTERIES: ARCHITECTURE AND PLAN. There is a lack of general treatises on this subject; but the account of monastic architecture by C. Enlart, *Manuel d'Archéologie française*, Paris, 1904, II, 1–57, applies, *mutatis mutandis*, to English monasteries, and contains a general bibliograhy.

The foundation of the study of the Benedictine plan was laid down by Professor Willis in his articles on *Worcester Cathedral and Monastery* (*Archaeol. Journal*, vol. XX), and in *The Architectural History of the Conventual Buildings of the Monastery of Christ Church in Canterbury*, 1869. D. J. Stewart's *Architectural History of Ely Cathedral*, 1868, is another remarkable work of the same period. Other important works are J. T. Micklethwaite's *Notes on the Abbey buildings of Westminster* (*Archaeol. Journal*, vols. XXXIII, LI), Sir W. H. St John Hope's *Notes on the Benedictine Abbey of St Peter at Gloucester* (*Ibid.* vol. LIV) and *Architectural History of the Cathedral Church and Monastery of St Andrew at Rochester* (reprinted from *Archaeol. Cantiana*, 1900), the accounts of Peterborough abbey by C. R. Peers (*Vict. Co. Hist. Northants*, vol. II), of St Albans abbey by C. R. Peers and W. Page (*Ibid. Herts*, vol. II) and of Winchester cathedral priory by C. R. Peers and

H. Brakspear (*Ibid. Hants*, vol. v), and W. H. Knowles' *Tynemouth Priory* (*Archaeol. Journal*, vol. LXVII). F. Bond's *Westminster Abbey*, 1909, is an admirably written and well illustrated volume.

The Carthusian plan is treated by Sir William Hope in *Mount Grace Priory* (*Yorks. Archaeol. Journal*, vol. XVIII, with historical articles by H. V. le Bas and W. Brown) and in *The London Charterhouse and its old water supply* (*Archaeologia*, vol. LVIII).

The peculiarities of the Cistercian order have received much attention: see E. Sharpe, *Architecture of the Cistercians* (*Journal R.I.B.A.*, 1870–1, pp. 189–210), and J. T. Micklethwaite, *Of the Cistercian plan* (*Yorks. Archaeol. Journal*, vol. VII). The chief monograph on the Cistercian plan is Sir William Hope's *Fountains Abbey* (*Yorks. Archaeol. Journal*, vol. XV, reprinted separately, 1900), and to the same writer's *Kirkstall Abbey* (*Thoresby Soc. Publications*, vol. XVI) is added an essay by J. Bilson on *The Architecture of the Cistercians*, reprinted, with some alterations, in *Archaeol. Journal*, vol. LXVI. It may be noted that Sir William Hope, among other discoveries, established for the first time in his *Fountains Abbey* the use of the Cistercian nave as the quire of the *conversi*, the arrangement of the Cistercian kitchen, and the fact of the disappearance of the *conversi* from Cistercian houses after the middle of the fourteenth century. He has further discussed Cistercian arrangements in *The Abbey of St Mary in Furness* (*Cumb. and Westm. Antiq. and Archaeol. Soc. Trans.*, vol. XVI, reprinted 1902), and with H. Brakspear in *Beaulieu Abbey* (*Archaeol. Journal*, vol. LXIII) and *Jervaulx Abbey* (*Yorks. Archaeol. Journal*, vol. XXI). Mr Brakspear's monographs include *On the first Church at Furness* (*Lanc. and Chesh. Antiq. Soc. Trans.*, vol XVIII), *The Church of Hayles Abbey* (*Archaeol. Journal*, vol. LVIII; see also *Bristol and Glouc. Archaeol. Soc. Trans.*, vol. XXIV), *Pipewell Abbey* (*Assoc. Archit. Soc. Reports*, vol. XXX), *Stanley Abbey* (*Wilts. Archaeol. Journal*, vol. XXXV), and *Waverley Abbey* (*Surrey Archaeol. Soc.*, 1905). See also R. W. Paul, *The Church and Monastery of Abbey Dore* (*Bristol and Glouc. Archaeol. Soc. Trans.*, vol. XXVII).

For Cluniac plans see Sir William Hope's *Architectural History of the Priory of St Pancras at Lewes* (*Archaeol. Journal*, vol. XLI; see also *Sussex Archaeol. Collections*, vols. XXXIV, XLIX) and *Castleacre Priory* (*Norfolk Archaeologia*, vol. XII).

The chief monographs on houses of Augustinian canons are the same writer's *Repton Priory* (*Derby Archaeol. Soc. Trans.*, vols. VI, VII; *Archaeol. Journal*, vol. XLI), the article by him and Mr Brakspear on *Haughmond Abbey* (*Archaeol. Journal*, vol. LXVI), and R. W. Paul's *Plan of the Church and Monastery of St Augustine, Bristol* (*Archaeologia*, vol. LXIII). See also J. W. Clark, *Observances of Barnwell*, ut sup., C. C. Hodges, *Hexham Abbey* (sic), 1888, and the learned series of articles by J. F. Hodgson on the plans of Augustinian churches (*Archaeol. Journal*, vols. XLI–XLVIII). Mr Brakspear has described two houses of Augustinian canonesses, viz., *Burnham Abbey* (*Ibid.*, vol. LX; see *Bucks. Archit. and Archaeol. Soc. Records*, vol. VIII) and *Lacock Abbey* (*Archaeologia*, vol. LVII; see also *Wilts. Archaeol. Journal*, vol. XXXI). The present writer has written an historical and architectural account of *The Priory of St Mary of Newstead in Sherwood Forest* (*Trans. Thoroton Soc.* vol. XXIII).

The Gilbertine plan is elucidated by Sir William Hope in *The Gilbertine Priory of Watton* (*Archaeol. Journal*, vol. LVIII).

Sir William Hope is further responsible for a series of articles upon various Premonstratensian abbeys, viz. Alnwick (*Archaeol. Journal*, vol. XLIV; see also *Archaeologia, Aeliana*, vol. XIII), Dale (*Derby Archaeol. Soc. Trans.*, vols. I, II), St Agatha's (*Yorks. Archaeol. Journal*, vol. X), St Radegund's (*Archaeol. Cantiana*, vol. XIV), Shap (*Cumb. and Westm. Antiq. and Archaeol. Soc. Trans.*, vol. X) and West Langdon (*Archaeol. Cantiana*, vol. XV). See also J. F. Hodgson, *Eggleston Abbey* (*Yorks. Archaeol. Journal*, vol. XVIII).

For the plans of friaries, see Sir William Hope's *On the Whitefriars or Carmelites of Hulne* (*Archaeol. Journal*, vol XLVII) and A. W. Clapham, *On the Topography of the Dominican Priory of London* (*Archaeologia*, vol. LXIII).

The above list embraces the most important contributions to the subject made during recent years. Many plans of other monasteries with brief descriptions will be found in the accounts of the summer meetings of the Royal Archaeological Institute in recent volumes of the *Archaeol. Journal*, and there are also plans of the chief monasteries in various volumes of *The Builder*. Sir William Hope's plans of Durham are given in *The Rites of Durham*, ut. sup. For further plans, see the topographical sections of the *Victoria County History* and the *History of Northumberland* (now in progress).

Historical monographs on religious houses, in which attention is paid to plan and architectural features, should not be forgotten. As examples of these may be cited S. O. Addy's *Beauchief Abbey*, Dr W. de Gray Birch's histories of *Neath Abbey* and *Margam Abbey*, C. Lynam's *Croxden Abbey*, and S. W. Williams' *Cistercian Abbey of Strata Florida*. Guide-books are not as a rule very trustworthy, but the official guide-book to Tintern abbey, for the architectural part of which Mr Brakspear is responsible, and F. Bligh Bond's guide to Glastonbury abbey are among the notable exceptions.

Articles of great historical value will be found under various headings in Smith's *Dictionary of Christian Antiquities*, the *Encyclopaedia Britannica* and the *Catholic Encyclopaedia*. It is unnecessary to refer to these in detail.

INDEX OF PERSONS AND PLACES

N.B. The name of each place in this list is followed by that of its county, or, if not in England, of its country, department or province. The description of the religious house as abbey or priory follows where necessary, and its order is added in brackets. Aug. = Augustinian; Ben. = Benedictine; Carm. = Carmelite; Carth. = Carthusian; Cist. = Cistercian; Clun. = Cluniac; Dom. = Dominican; Gilb. = Gilbertine; Prem. = Premonstratensian; Tiron. = Tironensian

www.ingramcontent.com/pod-product-compliance
Ingram Content Group UK Ltd.
Pitfield, Milton Keynes, MK11 3LW, UK
UKHW042144280225
455719UK00001B/98